BEING FAMOUS

BEING FAMOUS

Prepare **NOW** In The Dark For A Life In The Spotlight

ZAP RATH

Benjamin
BOOKS

BENJAMIN BOOKS HOLLYWOOD

A PIT TO PALACE PRODUCTION

Publisher's Cataloging-in-Publication Data
Provided by Five Rainbow's Cataloging Services
Names: Rath, Zap. | Marin, Murilo, illustrator.
Title: Being famous : prepare now in the dark for a life in the spotlight / Zap Rath ; [illustrated by] Murilo Marin.
Description: Hollywood, CA: Benjamin Books, 2017. | Includes bibliographical references.
Identifiers: LCCN 2016961723 | ISBN 978-0-9983684-0-5 (pbk.) | ISBN 978-0-9983684-1-2 (Kindle ebook) | ISBN 978-0-9983684-2-9 (PDF)
Subjects: LCSH: Fame--Social aspects. | Mass media and culture. | Popular culture. | Vocational guidance. | BISAC: SOCIAL SCIENCE / Popular Culture. | YOUNG ADULT NONFICTION / Careers.
Classification: LCC BJ1470.5.R38 2017 (print) | LCC BJ1470.5 (ebook) | DDC 306--dc23.
LC record available at http:lccn.loc.gov/2016961723

Printed and bound in the United States of America

ISBN: 0-9983684-0-7
ISBN-13: 978-0-9983684-0-5

Interior Illustrations: Murilo Marin (www.behance.net/bbxinterativa)
Cover Design: Zap Rath (www.zaprath.com)
Cover Photo: Joe Ankenbauer (www.joeography.co)
Cover Photo Editing: Bernard Wolf (www.bernardwolf.com)
Cover Photo Studio: Astroetic Studios (www.astroeticstudios.com)
Cover Photo Hairstylist: Chris Anthony (Instagram/Twitter: @sirchrisanthony)
Cover Photo Characters (from left to right):
       Bodyguard: James L. Nichols, II (www.imdb.me/JamesLNicholsII)
       Talent Agent: Saladin (www.facebook.com/saladin.florence)
       Fan #2: Chyna Monae Williams
       Celebrity: Jacob Tasher (Instagram: @jacob_tasher)
       Hairstylist: Angela Orosco
       Fan #1: Scharlanea Rae Cleveland
       Police Officer: Al Burke (www.mroutrageous.com)
       Paparazzo: Charles Chudabala (Instagram/Twitter: @cchudabala)

DEDICATION

This book is dedicated to my mother Rosa Benson who has always sacrificed her dreams so that I could chase mine; to Mary and Wesley Hanks, the unofficial godparents who made sure I at least looked famous; to Brother Gil Melendez who showed me the incredible power of connecting my spirit to my skills; to Earl Middleton who has always been there to cheer my merited steps and challenge my missteps; and to Dr. Deborah Fowler who has kept me straight enough to restore my integrity and push me into a greater destiny.

These people expect great things from me, and I cannot, I will not let them down.

DISCLAIMER

This book contains ideas and opinions of the author and is designed to provide helpful information regarding common issues and problems that the author has encountered. The author and publisher are not engaged in rendering medical, health, psychological, vocational, financial, commercial, or any other personal or professional services. We encourage you to consult with a competent professional before drawing any inferences or applying any concepts contained herein. In addition, references have been provided only for informational purposes and do not constitute endorsement of any source. Everyone is different, and some applications or advice from this book may not be suitable for your particular situation.

The author and publisher make no expressed or implied warranties or guarantees regarding any of the contents of this book and are not responsible for any loss, risk, liability, negative results, or damages, including but not limited to incidental, special, consequential, or any other damages, personal or otherwise, which occurs as a consequence, directly or indirectly, to any person reading or following any action, practice, treatment, or preparation suggested within this book.

Finally, both the author and publisher have made best efforts to ensure that the information contained herein is accurate at the time of press. However, the author and publisher also do not assume any liabilities regarding the completeness or accuracy of the book, contents, and specifically disclaim any implied liability or warranties to any party regarding omissions, errors, merchantability, or fitness of use for any particular purpose.

CONTENTS

INTRODUCTION

We live in an age where the concept of being famous has taken center stage in our society. Television is blanketed with reality shows, talent competitions, and exposés. News programs and publications now take their lead from gossip reporters who pry into the most personal realms of celebrity life. Tell-all books break the magician's code and reveal the puppet masters who pull the strings in the shadows behind the stars. The internet has flung open the doors of information and free expression before a worldwide audience. And, as a result of this fame focus, a predilection, or dare I say, an obsession with fame has reached a critical status.

If you have picked up this book, then I know that you must sense something within yourself as well. Perhaps you are an actor, a dancer, a writer, an artist, or a musician. Maybe you are a businessman, a chef, an athlete, a politician, or a church leader. Despite which route you take, the desire is still the same. It is that longing to be somebody great, to do something that draws attention, and to enjoy the trappings that seem to always surround the famous.

The advent of television, the extent of cable and satellite programming, the phenomena of reality television and televised talent competitions, and a future which is certain to contain even more interactive television have all contributed to informing and especially misinforming the public about the famous lifestyle. The *ordinary* man is being paraded across the airwaves right alongside the dedicated celebrity. At the time of this writing there have been over 1,000 reality televisions shows that have aired, and the numbers continue to grow as new content is constantly being produced to further feed the fame epidemic.[1] To put that astronomical number further into perspective, if you watched reality television show episodes 24 hours a day at an average episode length of 1 hour and an average season length of 20 episodes, it would take you over a year and a half to watch only 1 season of each show! These types of shows continue production because the ratings are so significant. In the 5th season of American Idol alone, an average of well over 30 million viewers tuned in.[2] That's roughly the combined population of 17 of America's largest cities. It is no secret that television has greatly impacted the definition of fame and how it is achieved. There is an unprecedented saturation, competition has become increasingly fierce, and a new set of rules apply to anyone who is trying to break through the crowd of hopefuls.

While newspapers have been dying a slow and painful death, celebrity gossip magazines have been thriving until recent declines in sales. This slippage has been caused by more and more fans turning to the web and celebrity gossip television shows like TMZ, but business has still been booming for gossip magazines even during a recession. At the top of the celebrity magazine pile is People magazine, with a circulation of over 3.5 million.[3] In 2011, the magazine had advertising revenues of nearly 1 billion dollars, the highest amount for any magazine in America.[4] It's obvious that people not only want to be celebrities themselves; they also want to know every detail of a celebrity life. According to the New York Times, gossip-driven websites, television shows, and magazines comprise an industry now worth about $3 billion dollars.[5] Now, even standard news outlets still feel forced to follow the sensationalistic lead of gossip magazines in order to retain readership.

The Internet has also been a mighty force in making sure that we all are bitten by the fame bug. Never before have words and images propagated by any ordinary man with a computer been able to be seen around the world in fractions of a second. Usage of the Internet puts us all in the spotlight immediately. It is referred to as the World Wide Web for a reason, and anything you post online instantly puts you in a global public forum. Every social networking site you sign up for is devoted to making you famous. Facebook and Twitter alone open you up to an audience of 1.6 billion monthly users and growing![6,7] The average man now leads a celebrity life and the Internet has provided the necessary accessories to further his fame. Today, Facebook is the common man's tabloid where his latest gossip may be found, YouTube is his own television channel on which he may showcase his great talents, and Twitter is the speakers' podium behind which he stands to give insightful orations to the public.

Centuries ago, fame was reserved for warriors, royalty, and religious leaders. It then evolved to also highlight politicians, artists, and scholars. Now, anyone can be famous for just about anything! You can be famous for a great achievement, for achievement at an abnormal age, or for an achievement that is unprecedented. On the other hand, you can be famous for underachieving and be thrust into the spotlight seemingly by accident. You can be famous for harming or attempting to harm yourself or other people. You can be famous for your sensational behavior, your distinctive personality, or your display of public perfection. You can be famous because of your money, because of your family name, or because of your leadership ability. You can be famous for befriending other famous people, for talking about other famous people, or for being famous yourself. Even the great Kathy Griffin has proven to us that you can be famous for not being very famous!

From the printing press to the internet, each time we have made a technological leap, fame has leapt with it in further propagation and saturation. Each time, more and more people from the audience are allowed to come up to the stage. But if everyone's on stage, who is left to be in the audience? For anyone seeking fame today, it's not enough to be onstage. Everyone is onstage! Now, it's as if you have to build another stage on the stage in order to be seen.

Such incredible societal changes require a new perspective on the concept of fame. Today, we view each other more and more with a fame mentality, and I believe that we are all famous to some degree. Anything you do in the public forum contributes to your public life, and we all have a public life among circles of friends and/or crowds of followers that is increasingly visible. Fame is no longer just reserved for movie stars, musicians, politicians, or athletes. The soloist at the local church is famous. The little girl who bravely fought illness is famous. The coach of the high school basketball team is famous. The CEO of the company is famous. Now there are famous airline pilots, chefs, lottery winners, hunters, and investors. Even the crook who robbed the convenient store last night will be broadcasted on the news.

A society immersed in fame, however, is not a new phenomenon. The prominence of fame in the United States is eerily similar to that of the Roman Empire when public image was also regarded very highly. At that time, fame was only reserved for great rulers, warriors, orators, and other aristocracy. On the contrary, our current aristocracy now has to compete with a wide array of other attention-grabbers, and outside of the President and possibly his cabinet, most people don't even know who our government leaders are. Virtually anyone is allowed to get in on the act, and even the Flavor Flav's of the world who have more of a resemblance to a court jester than a great achiever, can be counted among the well-known. Our ability to produce, reproduce, and disseminate words and images in large quantities instantly and globally has turned us into a Roman Empire on steroids.

In the true paradoxical nature of fame, society is more connected and organized than ever before while simultaneously being more distant, cluttered, problematic, and confusing. Social networking sites have become the mirrors that show how narcissistic and desperate for attention we really are. The real connections are few and far between, and the sites have become the place where people are just allowed to peep through the windows of our lives. It's like we are all virtual exhibitionists collecting a database of stalkers. Our social accounts have very few friends, but a multitude of watchers.

It's not surprising to hear the number of people who claim that they are now addicted to social networking. Some (myself included) have abstained from the social networking sites almost as a religious fast to purge themselves of the life-enveloping "social" scene. The word *friend* has lost its meaning as hoards of people online have no real-life connection to the persons they have befriended. Socially, many people are much more awkward and introverted as they have traded reality for virtual reality. They walk around with headphones on their heads and computers or phones in their hands, cocooning in a virtual world of popularity and closing off their eyes and ears to the real world that is happening all around them. Several of these distracted people have run into other people or vehicles, causing serious injuries and even fatalities. But, when I peer over their shoulders, I see that they are endangering themselves and others in order to update a status, watch a silly video, or kill pigs with birds that for some reason are very angry.

For anyone who is left in the audience, there is no longer a singular focus. Most of us are onstage, and we all sound like an orchestra warming up. The symphony is not heard, and today there is only a cacophony of noise that is swallowing up some of our most worthy soloists. But, with the constant influx of fame seekers, it seems that more and more people who jump onstage also have no stage experience. Fewer people actually understand fame and how it radically transforms their lives. Today, fame has become an enticing career within itself, but droves of people make dangerous attempts at being famous without any structure or guidelines.

Depression, eating disorders, and identity crises run rampant as we constantly compare ourselves to other celebrities. Psychologists are now diagnosing celebrity meltdowns as a disorder called acquired situational narcissism, while the fans, a name that we must remember is short for fanatics, are developing what is now called celebrity worship syndrome. Others are struggling financially, sacrificing certain needs and wants in order to devote money to things that will perpetuate their fame. But, despite all of the negatives of fame, the positives seem so overwhelming that we continue the pursuit. Fame is actually a wonderfully fulfilling and purposeful experience, but as you'll see later in this book, it is less of a place and more of a doorway to other things that we value.

The road to fame, unfortunately, is comparable to the streets of Hollywood, full of broken dreams and broken people. The reality is that there are a few ways to succeed and a great multitude of ways to fail. Fame is often misunderstood as the experience is aggrandized on television. We fawn over the glitz and glamour, craving fame's desirable qualities while writing off the celebrity woes that fill the daily headlines as the antics of weirdos who just can't handle their newfound attention. Certain celebrity issues have become a revolving door as we see the same problems occurring with each new star who is thrust upon the world stage. From drug habits to money problems, mental breakdowns to unruly attitudes, we must recognize that there are some common issues that occur repeatedly among celebrities, suggesting that fame causes a level of susceptibility to or exposure of these specific life problems.

A famous life is much different from a normal life, and you must become aware of that change in intensity during your pursuit. Rapid change, especially between extremes is always problematic for human beings. Astronauts who come back from a lengthy space mission may take up to several years to reverse some of the physical effects of extended periods in space. When we slam on the brakes in our car, the rapid change of speed causes our bodies to continue to go forward even though the vehicle has stopped. When we step out of a hot shower into a cold room, we immediately begin to shiver as our bodies try to adjust to the rapid temperature change. Similarly, a rapid change occurs in the transitions between a normal life and a famous life.

Even after a single performance full of throngs of adoring fans, you may return to the loneliness, routine, and struggle of real life. That kind of drop-off takes you from 100 to 0 in a matter of minutes. If you're not prepared to handle an up and down life, you can really stumble and sabotage your career. On the roller coaster of fame, a few seem to handle it well while many others end up with motion sickness. Even worse, the ones who don't strap themselves in get thrown off the ride completely. Nevertheless, at the end of a fun ride on fame, the response is usually the same: "Let's do it again!"

Being Famous is a result of my childhood notoriety and my adult life amongst the stars in Hollywood. Growing up, everyone seemed to know me in my hometown of Montgomery, Alabama for my musical abilities. Fellow students, teachers, church members, neighbors, and city officials could tell you about me, whether I knew them or not. Thousands of people were aware of me at a young age, but that all seemed normal as fame at some level was the only kind of life I had experienced since the age of five. Although my personality revealed a strangely simultaneous alienation that evaded popularity, my talent continually became an attraction that resulted in fame.

When I became an adult, I eventually moved to Los Angeles. In addition to continuing and expanding my music performance, I also had various professional and amateur stints as a music director, music instructor, stage hand, audio engineer, record label assistant, music producer, comedian, rapper, marketer, salesman, dancer, actor, entrepreneur, and model. Through all of these artistic endeavors, I garnered an exclusive first-hand look into the lives of stars and aspiring stars whose fame superseded my own by leaps and bounds. I vigorously gleamed every tidbit I could learn from the famous and constantly educated myself in the entertainment industry for my own success in Hollywood. However, I never expected that my casual observations would be so incredibly helpful to truly understanding myself and my industry and sustaining my life in the spotlight.

Many have known me only as a musician, and if the list of my other activities isn't surprising enough, I now add author to my catalog of endeavors. Over the years, I have actually had many book ideas in mind, but this book was not one of them. This title came as a surprise to me, but the timing does make sense. This book was written after a period of crisis in my life during which I quit music and other artistic pursuits altogether. I was frustrated with the way my life was going, and I was confused by the results of my labors. It seemed that the harder I worked, the more I went nowhere.

I stopped trying to be myself over the years, and I was sucked into placating everyone else. Instead of trying to be innovative, I was trying to be imitative. I was spinning my wheels trying to be famous for so long that I not only burned myself out, I forgot why I was even trying to be famous in the first place. I began to see that my imitation of others was actually a jealousy that caused me to discredit a long list of my own noteworthy accomplishments. I soon learned that **imitation of others is often rooted in emptiness, while true inspiration from God is rooted in openness**. An overemphasis on my public life had also caused me to neglect my private life, and instead of being blessed by fame, I was constantly being burned by it. I didn't know how to handle fame even at its smallest degrees.

I would like to say that I had some great revelation that caused me to shut everything down, research the various facets of fame, and write this book, but that's not how it really happened. In actuality, my private life was falling apart so much that I was literally forced to confront my negligence and naiveté. I had to take a break from fame; my future depended on it. I didn't send out emails about what I was doing (like I had done often in the past). I didn't announce it on Twitter and Facebook. I just did it. This initially wasn't for the crowd; it was for me. I needed to take care of myself before I could help others anymore. It took nearly three years of research and reflection on my journey, but in that period of time, I learned much about the world and the nature of a life in the spotlight. It was during that time that I eventually came to the realization that if I was going to continue in the light, I needed to make some vast improvements to myself in the dark.

I had to go deep into the darkness in order to save my light, and my life transformation was so dramatic that I eventually compiled portions of my notes into this book in hopes that the rocky roads of others might become smoother as well. This book embodies my experience, and the lessons I share here are the results of years of fact-finding and nearly three decades in the spotlight to some degree. Every day is a struggle even though I am much better, but the fight to overcome seems to be a continual part of the human predicament. I believe there are some things which are beyond our language that we will never understand while we are here on this Earth. So, we have to make do and interpret life to the best of our abilities.

In the following pages, I will share with you what I have learned in hopes that by reading it you will have a better understanding of the issues that are most commonly associated with fame and thus, a better control of your own famous life. *Being Famous* is the book that I wish someone would have given me before I ever stepped foot into Hollywood. It is a compilation of the many stories you have heard in the news media, my own personal interactions from my work with celebrities and those striving for fame, and my own successes and failures during my pursuit of a life in the spotlight.

With my artistic background, this book is designed with artists in mind; however, it can be applied to anyone who is or aspires to be in a position of notoriety, whether it be with 10 people or 10 million people. In the text, I use the labels of *someone in the spotlight, star, celebrity, famous person, artist*, and so on, interchangeably. Just apply the words that best describe your current or anticipated status. You will also see various lines of text within the paragraphs that are formatted in a **bold font**. Those words are powerful key phrases that will quickly help you internalize some of the foundational concepts I present here.

Lastly, this book is divided into two sections: the darkness and the light. I use these two terms to describe the two worlds that must coexist in fame: the private realm and the public realm. In actuality, fame is a struggle-filled balancing act between personal and public, darkness and light, spirit and flesh. Correspondingly, this book also has two purposes. First, it is designed to help you understand the crucial role your personal life plays in supporting your public life. If there is one thing that we have gained from prying into the intimate realms of celebrities, it is the exposure of valuable lessons to be learned in regards to the effects of their personal successes and failures. These pearls of wisdom, however, are no good if we don't take the time to analyze the various components of identity, learn from the ones who are or were where we want to be, and apply the lessons in our own lives. Secondly, this book is designed to help you understand the modern-day concept of fame, its related issues and the various ways that it is achieved and sustained. In an ever-increasing fame competition, the rules continue to change, and those with the most cunning and the most resources are rising to the top. Meanwhile, the rest of the fame seekers live in a world of delusion in which their great, not-so-great, or non-existent talent alone will someday transform them into a household name.

In order to sustain in the light, you must succeed in the darkness. Darkness always has light; day always has night. We use the term *star* to describe a famous person, but in our comparison, we must remember that the literal star in the sky thrives in an environment of darkness. **An inappro-**

priate amount of darkness or light, private or public is always the reason for fame failure. Still, this idea of a dark counterpart to the spotlight is not new. It's almost funny that in our desperate attempts to become famous, we ignore the wisdom of the most famous person who ever walked the Earth: Jesus Christ.

Despite your religious belief, you cannot deny the fame of Jesus and the resulting faith of Christianity. But, in 33 years on Earth, he spent 30 years of preparation in the dark and 3 years in the light actually being famous on a high level. That's a 90% window of darkness in order to produce a 10% window of light! And even then, religious texts show us that he still made repeated retreats back to the solitude of darkness in order to replenish the energies that the light drained from him.[8] "Every person who successfully remains public protects himself by balancing an inner private world with the demands of the public audience."[9] If you truly want to succeed at fame, you must prepare in the dark for a life in the spotlight.

Being Famous is not a guarantee of any high level of fame for myself or anyone else reading this book. That is not the nature of fame, and anyone who would make such a claim is a swindler playing on the ego and desperation of the next fame-driven fool. Instead, as the subtitle suggests, this book is a preparatory tool that addresses 12 of the most common issues associated with a life in the spotlight: identity, physicality, mentality, spirituality, sociality, emotionality, private life structure, public life structure, the *it factor*, negative events, business basics, and money. This book is about strapping yourself in for the fame roller coaster and finding ways to overcome the wooziness so that you can continue to ride. By applying the lessons within, you will be able to frame your life for fame so that you can handle it at any level, and then shape your fame for sustenance so that you can maximize your time in the spotlight and capitalize on your visibility.

Works Cited

1 ("Reality TV World")

2 (ABC Television Network)

3 (Alliance For Audited Media)

4 (Flamm)

5 (Rutenberg)

6 (Facebook, Inc.)

7 (YouTube, LLC)

8 (*NIV*, Luke 5:16)

9 (Braudy 109)

SECTION I:
THE DARKNESS

1
THE CORE
OF
CONFUSION

Imagine that we have found a new planet inhabited by some of the most primitive alien life forms. Their advancement is only as far as our stone age, so when we bring automobiles to their planet, they are highly excited and intrigued (Don't worry, you are still reading the right book). The aliens have no understanding of cars, so they begin to use them in odd ways. One alien parks the car inside of his cave and uses only the headlights for interior lighting. Another alien uses it as a toy for the kids to play on. Some aliens use it as a home with sleeping quarters in the trunk. Some push it in the water and try to use it as a boat. Others only use the car horn as a musical instrument, and the ones who have figured out how to turn it on just leave it in park, revving the engine occasionally to scare away animals. They bang on the engine until pieces break off, and they fill the gas tank with pebbles and sand. Some of them even treat the car as sacred and worship it.

Now, what does this ridiculous alien story have to do with you? Well, everything! The aliens misused the car because they did not understand the car. The car had no clearly defined identity for them, so they just made up their own identities for it. They used it in whatever manner they pleased, regardless of the car's actual purpose or the consequences of misuse. This doesn't sound like a very smart thing for anyone to do, yet we act in this manner with our own lives all the time. We begin to work, play, speak, entertain, teach, plan, and basically use *ourselves* without understanding how we are constructed, what we like and don't like, where we fit in, what we believe in, how to take care of ourselves, what actions we are prone to, where we came from, and much more. This is why I believe that a clearly defined identity is the ultimate foundation for not only anyone in the spotlight, but for every person...or alien.

ACTION AND JUSTIFICATION
You need to understand your identity for several reasons. First, your identity

determines what you do and why you do it. Anything that you do in life starts with your identity and you cannot truly know what you are supposed to do until you know who you are. When you know who you are, then you have a fundamental purpose on which to build what you do. **We are most proficient when our person and purpose come before our pursuit**. The idea is that design comes before function. Julia Cameron, author of *The Artist's Way*, puts it like this: "…in order to have self expression, we must first have a self to express."[1] Ask yourself some important questions before you jump into a life of fame. What do you do? Are you a singer, an actor, a musician, a dancer, a politician, a speaker, a leader? Then ask why you do what you do. What are you attempting to achieve in the process? Do these things link back to your identity? Do they reflect who you are?

Consider another analogous example. A chair usually has four legs, a seat, and some sort of back support at a right angle. A bed may also have four legs, but is bigger and wider, with a mattress parallel to the ground. The bed is also typically covered with sheets and a pillow on top. Now, you could certainly use the chair for sleeping, but it is not the best way to get a good night's rest. Similarly, you could sit on a bed, but it would look pretty weird at the dining table. Why? Because, at the end of the day, a chair is not a bed, and a bed is not a chair. One is meant for sitting, and the other is meant for lying down. The chair is built to serve a specific purpose that the bed does not provide, and vice versa.

As a more topical example, when people ask me if I am a singer, I usually say, "I can sing, but I'm really a musician." I not only understand my vocal limitations but also the expectations of others in our new American-Idol society. I understand that I am a baritone, not a flashy tenor who can belt and do runs. I can hit all the right notes. I can even be a solid background singer for you, but that is not at the core of my identity. Now, I could make a thousand demos, schedule concerts, and advertise all over the city, but if I'm not really a great singer, my success will be mild because people will sense that identity conflict. **Remember, a hard hustle in the wrong direction will just get you nowhere fast**.

TIMING AND PLACEMENT

Next, your identity determines when and where you do what you do. It establishes the appropriate time and place for your purposes to be carried out. For instance, a comedian probably should not do his comedy routine during a morning funeral. Even though a comedic endeavor aligns with his identity, his timing is inappropriate. On the other hand, a comedian at a cosmic bowling birthday party has chosen a better time, but his location is still a bit odd. With a clear understanding, the comedian will choose times and places that are conducive to his purpose and will give him the best chance to succeed. When you clearly identify yourself, the *when* and *where* will fit with what you do.

Your timing and placement can also be understood as the environment you operate in, and the more specific you are with your identity, the more specifically you can define your environment. Imagine a fancy king size bed made with rich mahogany wood. It has down pillows and red satin sheets. Now, would you put this bed in a shack? No. The bed is so clearly defined that it demands a complimentary environment. The room and everything else in it should match the quality of the bed, or it will look out of place. It is the same with our lives. The specificity with which you operate will enable you to more easily decide who or what you should have around you in your environment.

MANNER

Your identity also determines how you do what you do. Basically, as you internally define who you are, you will begin to see how your external actions reflect you accordingly. Are you a stubborn boss? Are you a perfectionist? Do you write horribly? The more specific you can be with yourself, the better you can define yourself. Work backwards and really think about the way you do things. What does this say about your character?

The biggest way to get lost in the shuffle is to try to be normal. You are not like everyone else, so why try to be? The way you do things is unique to you. Recognize that and own it. Some of your identifying traits are developed, while others are innate. Recognizing the origin of and differences between each will be very helpful to you, so take ownership of your characteristics. And, if you don't like how you do things, then change and be consistent about it. Really get to know yourself. The more you know who you are, the more you know who you are not, and the quicker you will be able to make decisions. Businesses, for example are constantly solidifying their identity in the minds of their staff and their customers through the manner in which they do things. When you walk into Wal-Mart, you expect low prices. When you take a trip to Disneyland, you expect a magical experience. If these businesses did things any other way, it would create a confusion which would eventually result in distrust. When you are famous, your style, your approach, your unique way of doing things will all be traced back to your identity. And, when you do *it* like no other, you increase your potential for fame.

SURVIVING CHANGE

A strong identity is also important because it provides stability amongst change. Everything around us changes all the time. The weather changes, people change, and our circumstances change. Nothing in this world stays the same as it used to be, and nothing in this world will be the same in the future. With each passing second, something has changed, whether we see it or not. This is a reality that we cannot alter, so we must learn to live with change. And in the book, *The 7 Habits of Highly Effective People*, Stephen Covey points out that "people cannot live with change if there is not a changeless core inside them."[2] A strong identity is an anchor during those changes, so that we do not become unstable ourselves. Does your identity enable you to remain stable, or do you falter every time life throws you a curve ball?

Our development depends not only on ourselves, but also on others. The person who considers only his or her own thoughts and feelings is self-centered, and we all know people like this. On a larger scale, some of our favorite celebrities tend to be or appear to be self-centered. Some even surround themselves with yes-men who subjugate their own true feelings to the celebrity's self-centered motives. Self-centeredness also goes hand in hand with self-delusion. This happens when you "confuse the qualities that you want with the qualities that you truly have."[3] With this thinking, you are always right, and no one can tell you that you are wrong.

GAINING PERSPECTIVE

We can and should operate on a higher social intelligence level than self-centeredness, while still being self-aware. To obtain a more balanced perspective of life, you should take into consideration the thoughts and feelings of others along with your own perceptions. In any kind of performance endeavor, this is incredibly important. If no one can critique you, you absolutely will not get better. If someone hates your modeling photos, perhaps they are just a hater. Or, maybe you really should lose those 300 pounds that you just picked up! When you come out of yourself and see the perspective of someone else, allowing them to influence you, you now can influence them as well, and that is extremely powerful.

The perspective of others can be invaluable; however, as a word of caution, keep in mind that other people form your identity from who they *think* you are. Now, this may actually be because of who you are. It may be because of what you have done. Or, it may be unrelated to you completely and just a response from a distorted perception. You must remember that your own perception of yourself is the most important. This is not to say that you should ignore the perceptions of others, because sometimes other people can say things that allow you to see attributes within yourself that you did not recognize. Just make sure that you are also able to see what they say. Don't always take their word for it.

ARCHETYPES AND STEREOTYPES

Most people will also tend to think of you in generalizations. People build their perceptions about you based on what they see on the surface. We are very complicated beings, but we do not have the innate faculties to look at each other deeply. So, expect others to make general assessments in their brief interactions with you in order to form an identity perception.

The concept of archetypes is a great way to understand how people perceive you. An archetype is a standard literary tool for characterization in storytelling, and that translates well to the drama that is our life. Socialite, jokester, gym rat, and emo kid, are all examples of archetypes. They are very loose descriptions and can change to fit desires; however, they are not stereotypes. Stereotypes are oversimplified and offensive generalizations, normally of a particular group of individuals. They are people's attempt to have x-ray vision, based on distorted conceptualizations. To further understand the differences between archetypes and stereotypes, take a look at the contrasting definitions below.

1. Archetypes are standard ideas. Stereotypes are ideas that are held up as if they are standards.

2. Archetypes say, "Because you do, you are." Stereotypes say, "Because you are, you do."

3. Archetypes use blanket outer descriptions to summarize your inner qualities. Stereotypes take inner preconceptions and project them onto you.

Since people think in these broad characterizations, as someone in the spotlight, you must capitalize on your interactions with them by identifying with a key archetype that best represents you, thus giving them a solid starting point from which to understand you. The ability to convey who you are as quickly as possible is a very beneficial skill.

IMPLEMENTING ICONOGRAPHY

Another way in which you can quickly convey a summary identity is through iconography. Iconography is images, symbols, and other modes of representation that can stand for or be associated with a company, a movement, or even you! We are very visual beings, and the images that we see can have tremendous effects on us. The most obvious use of iconography is in our media. It is so important that companies pay thousands not only to create the perfect logo, but thousands to protect it while they use it.

Iconography makes it easy for a company to establish familiarity with its products and/or ideals. For example, sometimes I go to McDonald's just because I know how the food is going to taste. If I'm on the road, and I see a place that I have never heard of next to the golden arches, I'll probably take the golden arches. I don't even have to exit the freeway yet. I see the sign before I get there, and the iconography is so strong that I can almost taste the food before I eat it.

Iconography isn't just for products or movements. It can also do wonders for you as a person. In fact, iconography can associate people with products or even turn people into products. Our perception of the person immediately gives us a perception of the product, and this is at the heart of branding which we will discuss later. For instance, when you see the Michael Jordan silhouette of his famous dunk, with one arm extended and legs spread, you immediately get an impression of not only Michael Jordan, but also of the products he promotes. You may think to yourself, "Wow, he's talented. He's so athletic. He must have worked hard to be able to do that. Maybe if I buy his products, I can jump as high as he can." Look at the wealth of response a single image can generate. With iconography, I don't have to describe myself to you. I simply give you the picture and let your mind do the rest.

Iconographic Strength

If you can use iconography, there are two attributes that will help you become successful with it. First, your iconography needs to be strong. It needs to make an impact, and I encourage people who are not graphic artists to have a professional design their logos and other promotional materials. Graphic artists have been specifically trained to create imagery that is impactive, and if you are a know-it-all and do it yourself, you run the risk of portraying a weak image.

Iconographic strength can also be affected by financial resources. How would you perceive my business if I gave you a hand-written business card on a torn piece of notebook paper? Now what if I gave you a business card with my information printed with a fancy font on heavy duty card stock? That second example gives a much stronger impression. And just like that business card, anything else you create or associate with is an extension of you that further shapes your iconography in the public eye.

Iconographic Consistency

The second attribute that can propel your iconography is consistency. However, consistency requires integrity, and integrity means that what you do lines up with what you say. Consider the following scenario: Let's say I run a music store called...oh...I don't know, Guitar Center. I have used the word guitar in my store name, and all my advertising has guitars everywhere. One day you walk into my store and ask to buy a Fender Stratocaster. I reply to you by saying that we don't sell guitars here, only keyboards. My business wouldn't last a week. Why not? My iconography is inconsistent with what I do. With a name like Guitar Center, I'm not only expected to carry guitars, but to be a mecca of guitars with various models from which to choose. Similarly, you must always try to be consistent in whatever you are doing or being. Inconsistency will upset people and cause them to turn away from you. However, with strong and consistent iconography, people will remember you. And when people remember you, you start to become famous!

Iconographic Confidence

Once you are conscious of your identity, you must be confident in your identity. You have to go all in. This is who I am. If you are confused, you will confuse others, and your message will be diluted. You must be intentional about what you are doing. A life in the spotlight will require you to have guts. Sometimes you should take chances. "I hope," "I want to," "I'm trying to," and "maybe" are not the words of a confident person. "I am," "I will," and "I can" are the beginnings of confident statements.

There is a difference, however, between confidence in yourself and confidence in your ability. Confidence in yourself gives you the gusto to step out and do. There are so many talented people that you have never heard of. And, you will never hear of them until they have confidence in themselves. It's not a matter of how well they will do it?" The question is, "Will they do it?" Talent will take you far, but confidence will take you even further. **Talent will bring you to the stage, but confidence will put you in the spotlight**.

When you are afraid to step out and be yourself, you are in danger of becoming what Cameron calls a shadow artist. She defines shadow artists as people who are too intimidated to become artists themselves and instead choose to shadow declared artists. Shadow artists tend to be invested in other people more than themselves. Or, they may just hang around people who actually have the confidence to be and do what they want to be and do as well. It's very easy to slide into the life of a shadow artist, but continued confidence in yourself will help you get out of the rut.

Things can be even worse when you have no confidence in your ability. You may have the courage to go up on stage, but you have no faith in a successful outcome. When someone gets up on a stage and says, "I'm going to try and play this song for you. I don't know if it's any good, but I hope you like it," I usually leave before they start, because I'm certain that whatever is coming next is going to be god-awful. If you lack confidence, you will not perform at your maximum potential, and a lack of confidence in yourself will actually reduce other people's confidence in you as well. Having confidence doesn't mean that you are never scared. Everyone has fears, but the confident person acts despite those fears.

So, how do you become confident? Well, one big way to build confidence is through practice. It can be that simple. I have played music in front of 18 people, and I have played music in front of 18,000 people. Many ask me if I get nervous in either situation, and the answer is no. Why? Because before I touch that stage, I am always prepared. It's not rocket science. I have merely practiced my way into being comfortable. I have played the music over and over again without mistakes. Additionally, I have performed in front of people hundreds of times. Thus, I have practiced the experience, not just the music. It's easy for me now, and I don't even have to think much about the technicalities of what I'm doing. Preparation produces confidence, and with confidence you can just enjoy the moment.

■

Many of the news stories regarding troubled celebrities can be traced back to identity issues, and these kinds of problems can occur for many reasons. Doing the wrong thing, doing something for the wrong reasons, having the wrong timing, being in the wrong environment, or doing something in the wrong manner can all be destructive to your fame.

Knowing yourself is key to your stability and success, but it can be only half the battle as others can give you valuable insight from a different perspective. Still, you must remember that people's initial understanding of you will be through overall ideas and generalizations, using tools such as archetypes, stereotypes, and iconography. But strength, consistency, and confidence in yourself and your ability will enable you to project the best image and perform at a high level despite misinterpretations and unexpected circumstances.

In the next few chapters, we will expound on what identity actually is and break it down into five major interrelated areas: physicality, mentality, spirituality, sociality, and emotionality. Each area will be the foundation for a healthy life balance in which your fame can flourish and hopefully sustain the instability of life.

Works Cited

1 (Cameron 80)

2 (Covey 108)

3 (Flocker 21)

4 (Flocker 59)

2
FAME AT FIRST SIGHT

Your body is your most important asset and the most important part of your identity. Now, before you call me superficial, keep in mind that once your body dies, there is no more mental, emotional, social or spiritual direct influence that you can have on this earth. The body is the ultimate tool, as it allows for all your identifying qualities to function. And, you can become severely limited if you are physically unable to do what you want. Just like the aliens with their new cars, your physical component is a vehicle, and it requires knowledge for proper operation along with care and maintenance.

Since your body is your most visible representation, it comes under much scrutiny from yourself and others. So, body issues can be a source of insecurity, even when you are healthy. Fortunately, you are not stuck with every aspect of your body. There are numerous changes that you can make to enhance your perceived assets and reduce your perceived defects. With an understanding of yourself and the environment you will be operating in, you will be prepared to make changes that can improve your well-being and your fame.

KNOW YOURSELF

Health

Physical appearance can become a very touchy subject when in the limelight. For you to remain stable, you will need a solid core that is locked into your identity. The best approach for this core is to have a focus on health. You will look and feel your best when you are healthy. But, you shouldn't be healthy because I told you to be. You should be healthy because good health reflects who you are, because it's a part of your identity.

Many famous people become depressed, develop disorders, or even get sick and eventually die because of the pressures on their physical appearance. But, the fantasy world where everybody likes the way you look does not exist. When you are in the spotlight, you will always be scrutinized. The scrutiny will have nothing to do with your health on the inside, just your look on the outside.

Without a deeper perspective, people will see you in generalizations and project idealistic and unrealistic desires upon you. You're too fat. You're too skinny. Your hair is too long. Your hair is too short. Your clothes are too tight. Your clothes are too baggy. Someone will always find something wrong with you, whether it's valid or not. So, you should be confident in yourself and know what healthy means for you at the end of the day.

Genetics

Genetics is a big part of understanding yourself physically, and we all have strengths and weaknesses that make us unique. In fact, "...your genetic lineage may hold the key to the professional path best suited for you."[1] When it comes to using your qualities to your benefit, it is also best to think of strengths and weaknesses in a circular motion, instead of linearly. As a circle, strength has no beginning or end, and neither does weakness. In fact, the terms strength and weakness are just labels of qualities that you possess. And, a single quality can be a strength or weakness depending on your situation. If you are very tall, is that a strength or a weakness? Well, it depends. For a basketball player, it is a great strength, but for a jockey, it is a weakness.

Another key to physical success is constant growth. Anything that you do not maintain will fall apart. Anything that isn't growing is dying. You can't always depend on your good genes alone. The circle has no beginning or end, and you must continually develop your weaknesses so that they become strengths while developing your strengths so that they don't become weak.

LeBron James, for example, is one of the most amazing physical specimens in the game of basketball. He was just gifted with a genetic makeup that has elevated him athletically above his peers. Yet, he still works out, he still trains, and he still eats properly. He constantly enhances and maximizes his strengths, and that keeps him at the top of his game. That keeps him growing, or else he will decline.

In another example, Jared Fogle, forever known as the Subway guy, used to be an obese man. He had very poor health, including a bad diet, and that was a weakness for him. However, he began to exercise and eat healthier meals, so he lost a tremendous amount of weight. Now, he has achieved fame and fortune by doing commercials related to his success story. He worked on his weakness and now it is his strength. Remember, both weaknesses and strengths can be made stronger and used to your advantage.

Aging

Aging is another part of your physical reality that must be taken into consideration. There's nothing worse than a 40-year-old man trying to look and act like he's 20. And, a 16-year-old girl who tries to act like she's 30 is no better. The aging process is an added element beyond our control that puts time limitations on our strengths and weaknesses. That is why it is important to strike will the iron is hot. **Time is fame's greatest enemy**.

In your quest for fame, you must consider your age. There are some things that simply require an early start. For example, activities like sports, dancing, and music are picked up much better earlier in your life. You have some strengths at age 20 that will be weaknesses at age 40, not because you did not develop them, but because the aging process has altered you. But, if at 40 you have a 20-year-old mindset, you can find yourself desperately trying every pill, every surgeon, every style of clothing, and every haircut to get your "strength" back. However, if you accept the aging process and have a mindset that compliments your age, acknowledging your current place in life, you will find that you have a whole new set of strengths that aging has given you to replace whatever you have lost. "I'm too old" is a limiting, negative statement, a useless cognitive effort. If you are too old for X, that means that you are just the right age for Y. Concentrate on Y.

Body Language

Lastly, it is important to know that your body is not only a necessary vehicle, but also a telling communication tool. Now, when you think of communication, you usually think of speaking with words, but your entire body can actually communicate more than your mouth can. Experts say that nearly 60% of your communication can come from your body language.[2] Your posture, the way you walk, your facial expressions; they all tell others what is going on inside of you. Even the clothes that you wear help others develop a perception about you.

When a scantily clad girl walks with a strut, she is communicating that she is confident in herself and that she feels sexy. When a person's movements are stiff and erratic, their head on a swivel, we can easily sense that they are lost or looking for something. Going back to the identity concept, your communication verbally or physically should line up with who you are in order to give everyone the clearest perception about you. Our body language can be very natural, and many times we cannot hide our true selves behind it like we hide behind our words. And, your words may not be trusted if your body language does not coincide.

I use the concept of body language often when I work with singers. The amateur singer sings a song, but the professional singer communicates a song's meaning and uses their entire body to do so. If you are singing a happy song with a sad face, it sends a mixed message to the audience. If you are at the climax of a song, but your hands are by your side, your knees are locked together, your feet are nailed to the floor, and your eyes are up at the ceiling, you are communicating fear, not the power of the song. When your body lines up with the rest of your identity, your communication is very effective, and that opens the door for you to influence people.

KNOW YOUR ENVIRONMENT

Physical Preparedness

In whatever you plan on doing to be famous, you can maintain a high level of operation if you understand your environment and physically prepare for it. This sounds elementary, but many people tend to fall apart after years of toiling and focusing only on the task while neglecting the tool. You can physically prepare yourself by understanding the nature of your industry.

Touring, for instance, looks like fun, but life on the road can be harsh. Proper rest and even stricter exercise and diet regimens are essential, otherwise you can very easily burn out. If you are a singer or actor, you should prepare for extensive use of your vocal cords above and beyond your normal speaking voice. You simply cannot be the screaming fan at the baseball game the night before your big show. And, you will need to pass on that phlegm-causing ice cream cone right before you go on stage. Being famous puts abnormal stress on the body, so to obtain peak performance, your maintenance will also have to be above average. You cannot do your best if you do not prepare your body to handle the stresses of a famous life.

The spotlight is intense, and your care for yourself must match that intensity. The more you do, the more you must pay attention and take care of yourself. If your body is your vehicle, there is a difference between driving to the store twice a week and hauling freight across the country daily. The latter experience is more extreme, so your vehicle will require more attention and maintenance to safely make the trip.

Physical maintenance was a big problem for me in the past. I would run my engine hard, but I would not maintain myself properly. My negligence made me forgetful, tired, sick, unhappy, unfocused, and more. There were so many ways to maintain myself, but I would make excuses for my neglect. I would tell myself that I was young enough to handle it, that I didn't have the time, and that it cost too much to maintain. But, when it comes to keeping yourself healthy, you must find a way to make it work.

There are several ways to prepare yourself physically for the rigors of fame. Visits to the doctor and dentist are essential. If your business is stressful, you can practice various relaxation methods like meditation or spa treatments that will help you stay balanced. A proper diet can do wonders for you. An exercise regimen that keeps you limber, lean, and muscular can make the day-to-day life events much easier to handle. Maintenance is key to continual high-level performance. If you want to succeed, you need to prepare, but if you want continual success, you need to maintain.

Supply and Demand

The success you have with your physical appearance can be greatly affected by the needs of the specific industry in which you work. For example, I used to have a mohawk, ear piercings, and a beard, but when I began doing work for television, all the networks were doing serious dramas and cop shows, and my look became less desirable. So, what did I do? I shaved the mohawk to a low natural cut, I took out the earrings, I trimmed the beard, and I even lost weight to fit more typical sizes. After that, I looked the part and became more in demand because of the changes I made to my physical appearance. It is the simple law of supply and demand, and the more specifically you fit a demanded role, the more you will be sought after.

KNOW YOUR PATH

Evaluate Yourself

To use your physical appearance to your benefit, you must know and be realistic about what you do and do not have. Seriously evaluating your characteristics will enable you to identify archetypes that can give people a general idea about you. You can then factor in things like health, age, and genetic strengths and weaknesses to mold your persona.

The outer influences of stereotypes are often looked upon negatively, but they can help you if you use them properly. And, proper use comes from understanding people. If you know how others think, then you can find better ways to influence them. It's natural for people to group things together so that they can understand them. For example, the stereotype about modeling is that you have to be tall and thin, surviving only on celery and carrots. But although thinner models are most popular, there are all types of modeling for all shapes and sizes. Additionally, a model's diet while usually still healthy, can be much more diverse. Knowing these stereotypes when trying to fit a specific role can prepare you for acceptance or rejection.

Whether we realize it or not, we make so many associations based on appearance. When we see good teeth and hair, we think of news anchors. And have you seen the weather girls lately? They tend to be incredibly attractive with big busts, and that's not just a coincidence. If a guy has a thick mustache, we envision an evil tyrant. A thinner mustache reminds us of a creeper or a porn star. And, think about this: When is the last time you saw a U.S. President with a mustache? No president has worn one in over 100 years because in this visual age, looks matter. Although your own personal expression should be paramount, fame may require you to change yourself in order to use outer perception to your benefit.

Decide

When evaluating the manipulation of your strengths and weaknesses, it is important to make a distinction between your private life and your public life. We'll discuss this further in the book, but I bring this up here because getting the most out of your physical appearance usually involves maximizing your positive attributes and minimizing your negative attributes. This works fine in public, but in private, minimization is the road to neglect, and it can cause serious problems for you down the road. In private you should really be working on your weaknesses and trying to turn them into strengths.

List all of your physical strengths and weaknesses. Can you enhance any of your strengths? Can you hide your weaknesses in public while you work on them in private? Or, are your weaknesses natural traits that you are unable to change? These are the kinds of questions you should ask about your key physical traits in order to determine how you convey them.

Factor In Your Style

Your sense of style also comes into play in regards to your outer traits. Style is important, and it can be defined as a distinctive manner of expression.[3] It is eye-catching, immediately drawing attention to you and conveying who you are and what you associate with. Style, however, can be very individualistic these days, and sometimes you must do a little research or trial and error to find out what works for you.

Go out on a limb and try something different. If you look too nerdy, maybe you should ditch the glasses and try contacts. If you are too wild, go for a more conservative haircut. If you want to look more trendy, update your wardrobe at the latest fashion hotspot. If you are too boring, accessorize! If you are single and looking, go to a spa and get a makeover. If you are too flabby, tone up. If you're too defined, wear looser clothing. Once you have made internal decisions, really put some time and effort into your style. It is the bait on your hook, the outer layer that makes a first impression with people.

If you are like me and sometimes have no sense of style, pick up a magazine! Look at the people *who look like you*, and learn from them. When you are first starting out, there is no need to re-invent the wheel here. What messages are they sending with their physical appearance? Is it a message that you are trying to communicate as well? You don't have to copy them exactly, but you can get ideas and pick up tips from them.

Advertisements really helped me with my wardrobe. I didn't know how to match colors, so I used to wear a lot of black because it was easy. However, creativity is one of my strong qualities, and a more colorful wardrobe accentuates that. So, I looked at magazines and billboards, envisioning myself in the same clothes. I researched skin tones and the colors that best compliment them. I made a few select purchases here and there, and now people compliment me on my clothing choices. Whether it's a minor adjustment or a major overhaul, there are many ways to enhance your style.

Create Ways To Get There

Once you have assessed the various areas of your physical being, including but not limited to environment, outer perceptions, strengths and weaknesses, and style, you can begin to craft a game plan to shape yourself physically and reach your maximum fame potential. Diet, exercise, skincare, spa treatment, massage, surgery, clothing, accessories, hairstyles, piercings, and tattoos are all ways in which people maintain or change their bodies in a way that allows them to thrive in the spotlight.

Again, the ultimate rule of thumb regarding any of these items is health. Anything harmful to you may reduce your life span, thus limiting your fame and the amount of time you have to be physically impactful. Since your body is your biggest asset, you should carefully evaluate the risks you take with it. Also, try to avoid the quick fix, because that route often carries the highest risks. For example, work on your diet and exercise before you pop a miracle weight-loss pill. There is a reason why the tried and true methods are in fact tried and true. They work! As we explore the various physical change agents in the following pages, evaluate yourself and determine what you can implement for the improvement of your own life.

10 Ways To Improve Your Physical Appearance

1. Diet
When people want to lose weight, they automatically think exercise, but diet is a huge part of staying in shape. Some even say that losing weight is up to 80% diet and 20% exercise. Although things have changed over the years, the basic ideas regarding food intake are still the same. Fruits, vegetables, lean meats, dairy, and whole grains should be priorities while carbohydrates, oils, fats, processed food and other junk foods should be eaten in moderation.

If you have not been in school for a while, you may not have noticed that the food pyramid has also changed. The new model contains more specific information on the types of food and serving size, recommending serving sizes based on caloric intake. It also includes a physical fitness component. Instead of a pyramid, the plate model is the new visual representation of proper portions at each meal. For more information, you can visit www.choosemyplate.gov.

In addition to weight loss, proper diet can also reduce the stress of a life in the spotlight. Chef Akasha, who has cooked for Michael Jackson, Angelina Jolie, Barbra Streisand, Billy Bob Thornton, Pierce Brosman, and others explains, "Most celebrities work real hard—sometimes getting up at 4:00am, working fifteen to seventeen-hour days. They just feel better when they eat healthy. They have more energy and endurance...My clients know that cooking and eating healthy is de-stressing."[4] So, when the pressures of fame start to get to you, consider your diet as an initial remedy. You can even release stress-reducing hormones by eating foods that contain vitamins C, B5, and B6, as well as calcium, magnesium, and zinc.

Lastly, your diet can also have a tremendous effect on your skin, most importantly your facial skin. When it comes to your body, your face is what is seen and normally remembered the most. So, it is absolutely imperative that you take care of it. Even though skin is often exposed on our hands, feet, arms, and legs, at the end of the day, we recognize one another by face.

The relationship between diet and skincare was an incredible revelation for me as I battled facial acne for years. I tried all kinds of products and drugs, but nothing worked for me. Then, I learned that yogurt ingested internally or applied externally was great for clearing up bad skin. I changed my overall diet, including yogurt for breakfast, and my skin has been clear ever since. I wasted a lot of time and money on the quick-fix remedies I previously warned you about, when I should have just changed my diet. A diet change was much harder, but the results were more than worth it. According to Arcona, former facialist to the stars, natural remedies are the way to go. She says, "When you take care of yourself in a natural way, using natural products, your skin remains radiant and glowing. That's what beauty is..."[5] And, after seeing the effects of yogurt, I have to agree with her. Below is a list of other natural items that are also good for the skin:

Chocolate - contains antioxidants, Vitamin A, and Vitamin E
Milk Products - smooth and moisturize via lactic acid
Honey - cleanses and brings moisture to the skin
Potatoes - contain potassium which brightens skin
Lemons - lighten the skin and balance pigmentation

Tomatoes - have anti-aging properties and antioxidants
Steam - opens pores, cleanses skin, and detoxifies

2. Exercise

There are numerous benefits to exercising on a regular basis. Exercise in general makes you feel better, and it helps you tackle the tasks of the day. It is an escape from the stress of life in the spotlight, refreshing both your body and mind. It can elevate your mood and make you feel sexy and confident. On the other hand, when you don't exercise, you can feel sluggish, tired, weak, stiff, depressed, stressed out, and more.

It is also important to balance your regimen so that you do not burn out from one form of exercise and so that you remain physically proportionate. Exercise should include some type of aerobics to keep your cardiovascular system healthy and some type of muscular resistance to keep your muscular system strong. You should also stretch before and after each session to loosen your muscles and prevent injury. Aerobics builds endurance, resistance builds strength, and stretching builds flexibility. You need all three for balanced physical fitness.

Your exercise regimen or lack thereof may be more revealing about you than you think because it takes a certain internal drive to produce outer qualities. In addition to being a significant component of first impressions, physical fitness also provides a window in which you can see the results of action over time. The time element is huge because it enables you to identify habits, not just a singular action.

Take notice of what each component of exercise builds and how it relates to inner character. Someone with the dedication to exercise and stay in shape tells me that they have will power to do what is best for health. It tells me that they have endurance and may not easily give up. It tells me that they may be flexible enough to work with me. Although these characteristics may not always directly correlate to your physical fitness, they can be the starting point for general assessments until you obtain more knowledge. At any rate, **physical health is an outer picture of inner decisions made over time**, and that will help people identify you.

Exercise should not be a chore, and I believe that the best way to exercise is doing something that you really enjoy. Be aware of your physical abilities and limitations and find something that you can get lost in. Personally, I am a big fan of sports. Whether it's tennis, basketball, soccer, football, or any other sport, when you are playing, you almost forget that you are exercising. It becomes an escape, not a labor. I used to hate running. I still do, to a degree, but I love playing basketball. I had always tried to lose weight using various aerobic activities. They worked minimally, but many times I dreaded doing the activity. However, an opportunity for me to play basketball regularly arose, and I really became lost in the sport. Each day, I wasn't going to exercise; I was going to play basketball. And over the course of a year, I dropped 60 pounds!

3. Massage
In addition to relaxing the body, a good massage benefits you in many ways. It calms your nervous system and lowers your blood pressure while reducing your heart rate. Massage can even positively affect your creative ability. Celebrity massage therapist Michelle Kluck explains,

> …often when you calm your body and quiet your mind, you allow yourself to open up to new ideas and thoughts. After a relaxing mas sage, many celebrities have told me that they can focus better, everything becomes clearer to them, and they can feel creative flow."[6]

For all the athletes and dancers out there, massage can improve your muscle tone, flexibility, and posture while relieving cramps and spasms. For singers, it focuses you on deep breathing. And, for models and actors, it can improve your skin quality. Massage is not just a girly thing. It is essential for any hardworking person in the spotlight, and it should be at least a monthly pleasure.

4. Other Spa Treatments
Another extremely important yet often overlooked key to physical wellness is water. Water is essential to looking and feeling great. It sounds so simple, but we fill ourselves with so many soft drinks, juices, and other liquids that we sometimes don't leave room for water. The amount of water that you should drink depends on many factors including age, gender, environment, and lifestyle; however, average recommendations are about 2 liters a day for women and 3 liters a day for men. If you begin incorporating proper amounts of water into your diet, you will see detoxification and revitalization of your skin, improvements in digestive health, reduction in headaches, improved joint strength and flexibility, enhanced energy, a decrease in weight, and possibly greater concentration ability and cognitive performance.

Putting water inside your body does wonders, but water on the outside really does the trick as well. In fact, the healing properties of water used externally is the foundation of spa treatment. The word spa is actually an acronym for the Latin phrase salus per aquam, meaning health from water! In ancient times, this health was gained primarily by soaking in natural hot springs, and our hot tubs today with a constant flow of heated water have the same effect. The combination of heat, buoyancy, and hydrotherapy is really the key. The heat from a hot tub warms your blood, which in turn lowers your blood pressure. It also provides deep relaxation for your muscles and temporary pain relief. The buoyancy factor is the relief that your joints need. As you submerge your body, the water takes over most of your body weight. This means that your joints are receiving a much-needed break from holding you up all day. Lastly the jet nozzles combine heated water with pressurized water to form pinpointed hydrotherapy to specific areas of your body. So, although it may be viewed as a luxury, a hot tub or Jacuzzi, or even a sauna which has many of the same benefits, can be a significant factor in your health, especially as you get older.

Facials and body treatments are also popular basic spa activities that really focus on the health of your skin. About every 30 days, your skin cells move from your dermis or your "true skin" below the surface to your epidermis, which is the outer layer of your skin. When the cells reach this point, they are dead, but instead of just falling away, these dead cells stick to your body, clogging your pores and hair follicles. This aids in the collection of dirt and debris and causes breakouts and unhealthy-looking skin. So, to counter this, we engage in the process of exfoliation which removes this dead skin. Exfoliation is an essential part of all facials and body treatments, which are basically facials for the entire body. The number of times you do this again really varies from person to person and depends on many factors. However, since your skin goes through this rejuvenation cycle every 30 days, a once-a-month treatment schedule is a good starting point.

5. Surgery

Cosmetic surgery has become another popular route for physical change. Surgery can be the best answer to critical physical issues, and I don't oppose it. However, the strength and weaknesses of your physical features can often be determined by flawed perception, and using surgery to fix every perceived flaw can go overboard. With this in mind, I do tend to view it as a last resort. My rule of thumb is that you should not use surgery as the easy way out of something that can be attained through a traditional or natural, yet harder process such as eating properly and exercising. The lessons are learned during the journey, not just at the end. Don't skip to the finish line, or you will miss out on the valuable learning process that will allow you to grow. Do you actually need a nose job, or do you really need to address deeper issues regarding a low self-esteem?

Converting to a healthy life requires a change in identity. When it comes to image adjustment, many fads fail because they are not about life change. **Being unhealthy is not an outer problem; it's an inner problem that is reflected on the outside**. Surgery can be a quick outer fix, but it avoids inner change. You may look beautiful on the outside, but if you are unhealthy internally, it will always manifest eventually.

6. Clothing

Clothing is a much better quick-fix way to enhance your appearance. Clothes, however, should be worn with your particular physical features in mind. They should convey your identity, not confuse people as to who you are. Don't just buy clothes because they look nice, or just because you saw someone else wear them. What do you want to hide? What do you want to reveal? Keep abreast of current fashion trends, but remember to dress your age. You can still make your own individual statements, but carefully pick and choose your spots as your choices will elicit public response.

Your body shape should be the starting point for clothing choice and a precursor to the consideration of other factors such as height, weight, and skin tone. Body shape refers to the general shapes that very broadly outline the physical proportions of your body. Common female shapes include the triangle for women who are larger at the bottom, the upside-down triangle for top-heavy women, the circle for women who are thick around the middle, the rectangle for less curvy women, and the iconic hourglass figure for women who have proportionate curves. Males also have the circle shape to describe heavy men, the rectangle shape for skinny men, and the upside-down triangle for men who can be described as athletic, stocky, muscular, or bulky. As you can see in Figure 2-1, some outfits will be more flattering for you than others depending on your particular build.

7. Accessories

Accessory items can also be an easy way to change your look very quickly. When it comes to these items, my first stop is always glasses. I love glasses, and I can have up to 10 pairs at a time. If you want to look macho, grab the dark shades. If you want to look trendy, pull out the big sunglasses. If you want to look smarter, wear the glasses with fake lenses. If you want to look older, use the bifocals. There are so many things you can convey with glasses. Who knew that you could reveal so much by hiding your eyes!

There are also many other accessories available to you. For example, a good hat can be the answer to a bad haircut. It can cover up that bald spot, and it can draw attention from a large or oddly-shaped head. There is a popular recording artist, for instance, who comes to mind because he always wears hats. They are very fashionable and iconographic, but they serve another purpose. This performer's head is a bit large, and those hats hide that. Other accessories used by the stars include canes (Charlie Chaplin and Fred Astaire), jewelry (Elizabeth Taylor and Lil Jon), scarves (Cameron Diaz and

BODY
★ SHAPES ★

CIRCLE

The circle shape describes people who are round at the middle. Although your first inclination may be to hide your belly with baggy clothes, don't do it. Instead, find clothes that fit (not too baggy or too tight). Black colors and vertical stripes will also give a slimming illusion, and an empire top can camouflage the stomach for women.

TRIANGLE

A person with the triangle shape is smaller at the top and larger at the bottom. With this shape, you want to minimize the lower half and draw more attention to the upper body. You can achieve this with a horizontal stripe top or any other kind of top that broadens or emphasizes the chest or shoulders. Contrarily, pants that are slimmer at the thighs and wider at the legs can make you look thinner at the bottom.

RECTANGLE

If your body is lanky, lean, or lacking curvature, you probably have the rectangle shape. While your waist should be kept tight and simple, clothes that flare at the top or bottom of your body are ideal. A solid belt; color contrast between tops and bottoms; and flowy, unobstructed clothing will break up your angular shape. Any kind of layering will also add volume to your body.

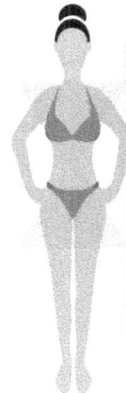

HOURGLASS

The coveted hourglass shape is a curvaceous womanly figure. The only way to mess up here is to show too much, show too little, or go overboard with accentuations. Don't let everything hang out, but don't get lost in boxy or baggy clothing either. Use clothes like crop tops, pencil skirts, one-piece outfits, and fitted jackets that emphasize your waist and flow naturally with your curves.

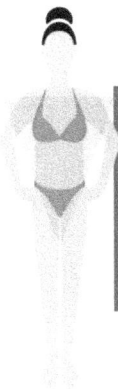

UPSIDE DOWN TRIANGLE

The upside-down triangle is a classic athletic shape that is wide at the chest and shoulders while being narrow in the lower body. Although this is a desired shape for men that can be complimented with horizontal stripes, straight-leg pants, or the classic v-neck, this shape can be troubling for top-heavy women. However, you can easily adapt if you just move attention to the bottom half. Any flowy, full-bodied, or long skirt or dress will work great. Wide-leg pants will also do the trick.

Figure 2-1

Nicole Richie), and even animals (Paris Hilton and DMX). You would probably be amazed at how many people you associate with their accessories.

8. Piercings and Tattoos
Piercings and tattoos are accessories as well, but their permanence, like surgery, puts them in a different category. Although piercings and tattoos are increasingly common for men and women, they still are symbols of edginess. So, if you are a bit bland, this alteration can add a more hardcore element to your appearance. These accessories usually have a significant meaning attached to them, so make sure that they line up with your identity. What are your boundaries? What is off limits? What are the health risks? These are the kinds of questions you should have answers to before altering your body. Also, consider the groups of people you associate with. How will your current boss, church members, business partners, or family view your tattoos or piercings? With any bodily alterations, even as accessories, it's wise to consider any long-term consequences that may negatively affect you.

9. Hairstyle
A great haircut can be so underestimated. However, as with clothing, you should choose a style that fits you, not just a style that is popular now. Just as your clothing choice should depend on your body shape, for the best hairstyle, you should choose a hairdo based on your face shape. The basic shapes include oval, square, oblong, heart, triangular, diamond, and round. Based on your face shape, there are certain hairstyles that will be more flattering for you. Other factors like your height or distinct facial features may also come into play. Be careful with toupées and wigs, and make sure you get it right. If you don't, you will just look awful. Finally, be wary of putting too many chemicals in your hair, many of which can cause you to lose your hair prematurely.

10. Smile
The internal and external benefits of a great smile are probably more substantial than you realize. And, your smile can attract fame all by itself. Lighting up a room with your smile isn't a myth. People are naturally drawn to someone who is smiling. On the other hand, if you frown or scowl, you naturally repel others. It doesn't take a rocket scientist to see which act is more conducive to fame. Follow the basic guidelines for good oral health. Brush and floss daily, get regular checkups, limit sweets and avoid staining and erosion which can be caused by coffee, colas, cigarettes, and other drugs. If your teeth are discolored or crooked, people will immediately make negative assessments about you. You need to make sure that your teeth are healthy, evenly spaced,

FACE
★ SHAPES ★

OVAL
The oval is considered to be the most attractive face shape. The forehead and jaw are the same width, and the face is a little wider at the cheek. The length of the face is also about 1.5 times the width of the cheeks. Just about any style looks good on the oval face as long as hair doesn't hang in your face or eyes.

The square face shape has roughly the same width at the forehead, cheekbones, and jawline, with the jaw usually being somewhat sharp. Long hair with textures such as choppy ends or curls are great for this shape. You want to avoid straight, heavy bangs that add angular lines or chin-length, blunt bobs that draw attention to the prominent jaw line.
SQUARE

OBLONG
The oblong shape is similar to the oval shape, but more narrow at the cheeks and/or longer from the forehead to the jaw. With this face shape, avoid long hair and hairdos that add height. These cuts emphasize the length of your face and possibly even make it look longer. Instead, try curly, layered, or wavy cuts to give the appearance of width. Bangs can also help you shorten the length of your face.

The heart face shape is wide at the forehead and narrow at the chin. With this face shape, you want to avoid short styles that highlight the upper half of your face. Side-swept bangs or wispy hair can help, and a chin-length style will add width to the bottom half. For men, a light beard can have the same illusion, adding some width that balances out the narrow jawline.
HEART

TRIANGLE
The triangle or upside-down heart face shape is wide at the chin and narrow at the forehead. For this shape, you want to add volume to the top half of the face. A shorter style with layers is often a good choice. Or, if you go longer, a soft wavy cut will work. Avoid heavy bangs and long wispy styles that flare out at the bottom. You want to pull attention to your forehead and away from your chin.

The diamond face shape is another long face that is very narrow at the forehead and jaw while being very wide at the cheekbones. For this shape, you want to add width to the forehead and jaw without adding height to the face. A shoulder-length bob works well, and any other feathery styles with soft lines and layers will diffuse your angular shape. Swide-swept bangs and deep side-parts are also good ideas.
DIAMOND

ROUND
The round face shape is roughly equal in width at the forehead, cheeks, and jaw. This is similar to the square shape, just more rounded and less angular. So, the goal here is to slim down the face a bit. Avoid big voluminous hair and curls. The long bob and other hairstyles that hang a little below the chin are great for this shape. Wispy or tapered ends will also add a helpful angular motion.

Figure 2-2

and naturally white in color, because people will notice your smile, especially when meeting you for the first time.

Studies show that individuals with great smiles are considered to be confident, successful, and attractive, which makes them much more likely to be approached or promoted to a higher position.[7] Even if you don't feel like it, smile. Believe it or not, your smile will actually trick your body into thinking that everything is OK. This has been linked to stress relief, mood elevation, lowered blood pressure, immune system improvement, and a more youthful appearance.[8] Don't wait for something to make you happy. Make happiness a part of you! Be happy. Even if you are sad, use a smile to force happiness in, and it will take its rightful place.

■□

A life of fame may appear to be a cakewalk, but on the contrary, it can be very physically demanding and stressful. Neglecting your body immediately shortens your fame, by shortening your life. It's so easy to get caught up in money, work, success, and all the other appeals of fame, but when your body is not at its best, you cannot completely be at your best. If you are a young person reading this, I know it can be difficult to understand the importance of maintaining your body, because it has probably never failed you. Your body, however, is the sole visible part of your identity, so you must protect it. It is the car that takes you throughout this world, and understanding factors like your current health status, your genetic makeup, the aging process, and your environment helps you prepare your vehicle for the journey that lies ahead.

Optimum physicality enables you to navigate through life much easier, which in turn allows you to focus on fame. And, once you have a handle on the product, you can then move your attention to the packaging. People's assessment of you usually starts with your outer appearance. From your clothing to your skin tone to your hairline, every part of your physicality is communicative whether you realize it or not. Fame has become increasingly superficial, and it is the outside that usually draws others inward, not the other way around. Consequently, if you neglect your outer appearance, you set yourself up to repel, not attract, inhibiting your fame by allowing people to move on to the next person who has invested in physical attraction. In this visual age, you can gain ground in fame by maintaining an attractive physical appearance. Manage what others see, but also allow your body to be a true reflection of how you see yourself.

Works Cited

1 (Flocker 35)

2 (Mehrabian)

3 ("Style")

4 (L. House and S. House 116)

5 (L. House and S. House 31)

6 (L. House and S. House 44)

7,8 (Stibich)

3 PROTECTION AND REFLECTION

HOW DO YOU THINK?

Your life is a very large and complex creation, so understanding your identity requires you to break down the big picture into smaller, more manageable pictures. I'm sure you have heard the famous Chinese proverb regarding this building-block process:

> Be careful of your thoughts, for your thoughts become your words.
> Be careful of your words, for your words become your actions.
> Be careful of your actions, for your actions become your habits.
> Be careful of your habits, for your habits become your character.
> Be careful of your character, for your character becomes your destiny.

To have control in your active life, you must start by maintaining control over your thought life. Your words, actions, habits, character, and destiny are all grown-up manifestations in the spotlight of baby thoughts that occurred in the darkness. Understanding this connection is crucial for any individual, but especially for those seeking fame. In the spotlight, you will be bombarded by many conflicting internal and external thoughts, and your destiny will be ruled by which thoughts you choose to accept or reject.

Mental Breakdowns and Psychological Disorders

The next component of identity is mental strength, and life in the spotlight requires an intense mental fortitude. To sustain mentally during fame, you have to handle overwhelming praise without becoming too arrogant, pressure situations without becoming nervous, widespread criticism without feeling defeated, constant failure without giving up, multiple duties without becoming overwhelmed, and the mandate to lead and explore without being afraid. This is an extraordinary life that necessitates continual evaluation of your mental faculties, because unfortunately a life in the spotlight puts you in a prime position to develop mental illness. Scientists have even made a connection between bipolar disorder and creativity.[1] This disorder, formerly called manic depression causes violent mood swings in addition to extreme highs and lows. The individuals listed in Figure 3-1 below have all struggled with mental illness. It truly is an issue that spans across a number of different famous vocations.

Politics[2,3]	Sports[4]
Tipper Gore	Mike Tyson
Winston Churchill	Terry Bradshaw
Calvin Coolidge	Delonte West
Princess Diana	Ken Griffey Jr.
Abraham Lincoln	Jerry West
Joseph Stalin	Zach Greinke
Music[5]	Art[6]
Robbie Williams	Vincent Van Gogh
Taylor Swift	Pablo Picasso
Selena Gomez	Georgia O'Keeffe
Brian Wilson	Michelangelo Buonarreli
Lady Gaga	Yayoi Kusama
Sinead O'Connor	Edward Munch
Writing[7]	Comedy[8]
Charles Dickens	Sarah Silverman
Edgar Allen Poe	Drew Carey
Leo Tolstoy	Ellen Degeneres
Ernest Hemingway	Conan O'Brien
Virginia Wolf	Robin Williams
Silvia Plath	Jim Carey
Film/TV[9]	Science[10]
Emma Stone	Leonardo Da Vinci
Clara Delevigne	Thomas Edison
Dwayne "The Rock" Johnson	Albert Einstein
Wayne Brady	Buzz Aldrin
Hayden Panettiere	Charles Darwin
Kerry Washington	Isaac Newton

Figure 3-1

Several people on the aforementioned list have even attempted suicide because of their mental issues, but you do not have to fall victim to public mental breakdowns or psychological disorders. If you are concerned about any mental conditions, I recommend evaluating your past and speaking with a trusted psychologist. If these types of issues are left unattended, they can reach a boiling point under the stress of a famous life and cause you to spin out of control in a very public fashion. The media eats up these kinds of train wrecks, and your mental health issues can become damaging to your career. In addition to professional help, below are some steps you can take to keep yourself mentally strong.

8 Ways to Build Mental Fortitude

1. Know What You Are Getting Into

Find out as much as you can about your industry or position before you step into it. Mental preparedness will give you a solid focus when managing the situations that may arise. For example, if you plan on being the next Beyoncé, you should know going in that you have a minimal 2.3% chance of success when it comes to just getting a record deal.[11] From there, you then have a 0.23% chance of actually being successful on that record label.[12] And, Beyoncé's success would be another level beyond that. To put those numbers in perspective, you are over 14 times more likely to be struck by lightning than to obtain a successful major label record deal.[13] This is just the reality of the music industry, and your mindset will be much different if you approach your task with this kind of realistic information.

2. Go To Sleep

Your mind becomes fatigued just like any other part of your body. It needs time to rest, and that is accomplished during sleep. In school, when everyone else was pulling all-nighters, I prepared myself mentally ahead of time, and coupled that with a good night's sleep before the test. It allowed for all the information I studied to sink into my brain, and I felt refreshed and ready to easily access the memory banks at test time.

3. Take A Walk

While you are building your physical appearance through diet and exercise, you are actually increasing your mental health. And, a simple walk can even be an effective means for clearing your mind.

4. Exercise Your Mind

What better way to prepare your mind for the challenges of life than to challenge it yourself! Writing with your less-dominant hand, solving brain teasers and puzzles, learning a new language, or reading something new and different will give you fresh perspectives while keeping your mind sharp and diversified.

5. Write

Writing is an amazing outlet for the mind. Thousands of thoughts fly through your head every day, even when you are trying to give it a rest during sleep. So, things can become cluttered and confusing inside your head. Writing organizes your thoughts and gives you clarity. It helps you figure out exactly what you are trying to say, and that is invaluable for a life in the spotlight where your words are heavily scrutinized. The process of writing this book alone has helped me tremendously in the management of my own life. The thousands of thoughts and questions in my head have been developed and analyzed through the research for this book, giving me helpful insights regarding my own situation.

6. Monitor Internal Thoughts

Your thought life truly has a major impact on your destiny. If you don't think it first, it doesn't happen. Fill yourself with positive thoughts, and get rid of any thinking that is negative or not useful.

7. Monitor External Thoughts

A life in the spotlight means that you will receive a barrage of other people's thoughts and opinions. Some will be constructive, but many will be negative or just completely unfounded, especially if you are doing something new and original. Recognize and separate the thoughts of others from actual facts. Then, stick with those facts and keep a positive attitude. **If one person's comment can bring you down, then you are not mentally ready for fame**.

You also must guard yourself when it comes to the media. From radio and television, to gaming consoles and smartphones, the media is the biggest time-draining machine of our era. New reports show that in our digital age, "the average American adult spends 11 hours per day with electronic media…"[14] This excessive media consumption not only atrophies your mind, it constantly reinforces your inadequacy through advertising. **Successful people do not watch television or play on the internet all day long**. Even many of the actors I have been on set with don't even watch the shows that they are acting in! If you engulf yourself in media, you will end up watching from the sidelines, not participating in the game.

8. Say Ummm

Meditation is a great practice with many benefits for your mental faculties. It increases stability, focus, peace, happiness, intuition, and more, while reducing stress, anger, anxiety, fear, and tension. Meditation also branches beyond the mind, influencing other components of your identity. It promotes spiritual growth and increases bodily health by lowering blood pressure, building the immune system, and improving vitality. In the Western world, meditation is more of a concentration on a particular person or thing in an effort to understand and/or heal. However, in the East, meditation is more connected to a spiritual ideal, not a thought process. It is about reaching a state of awareness and going outside of the mind. Either way, meditation can be a much-needed oasis in the desert of fame, and I highly recommend it.

WHAT DO YOU SAY?

The Power of Words

Your words are even more powerful than your thoughts. They give life and strength to what you are thinking. Words and thoughts also create a cycle that can expedite your elevation or your deterioration. For example, if you think you are dumb, and then tell yourself that you are dumb, you reinforce that negative thought, making it stronger. Or, if you think that you will do well and then declare that you will do well, you strengthen positivity. You can also weaken a negative or positive thought with positive or negative words respectively. The cycle continues when others hear what you say because they begin to internalize it, think it, and say it back to you. Now, you are thinking it and saying it, other people are thinking it and saying it, and whatever you are trying to achieve now has an incredible momentum fueled by a cycle of faith and positivity or an incredible impediment fueled by a cycle of doubt and negativity.

Motivational Mantras

A motivational mantra is the key to turning your negative beliefs into positive affirmations. This repetition of certain sounds, words, or phrases is often used as a tool to prepare for meditation, but it could even be as simple as a statement that you make when you wake up every morning. For instance, you could say, "Today is a good day. I expect good things to come my way." Even if the mantra is not true yet, it is still to be used as a way to speak your reality into existence. Mantras are very goal-oriented, and they enable you to speak the future into the present. Mantras also help a wandering or negative mind stay on track. If you can't stop thinking that you are ugly, your mantra then becomes, "I am beautiful." Reinforce your identity and inner values with motivational mantras and reap the benefits of positive self-talk. It will be a great counter to any internal or external negativity you may face.

WHY DO YOU BE?

Spirituality has become a prominent topic in recent years, and its various definitions have expanded. Some view spirituality as a path to purpose and meaning in life. Others view it as the discovery of one's true self, or one's role in life as part of the interconnection of humanity. I agree with those definitions, but I believe those ideas stem from a relationship with a supreme entity, a higher power greater than us, a creator, God, who guides our lives with spiritual principles. **Spirituality is at the core of your identity**. It determines your doing by giving reason to your being, hence the grammatically incorrect heading, "Why do you be?"

The Importance of Spirituality

Spirituality is an essential doorway to the darkness that will stabilize anyone in the spotlight, and it does a number of things for the fame seeker. Spirituality lifts you up when people are attacking you or tearing you down. Yet simultaneously, it provides an anchor to ground you when everyone else is puffing you up. I'm sure you have seen celebrities with out-of-control egos. It causes them to act out in selfish ways which eventually lead to inner and outer destruction. Spirituality counters this by bringing you to an awareness of your own frail humanity. It subdues your ego and shifts perspective to a broader picture. Spirituality also gives you the sense of purpose and meaning you need to drive you to overcome the extraordinary challenges that are unique to a life of fame. You will encounter obstacles far greater than the average person will ever face. When you no longer have control, a greater force will need to take over. And, unless you have made that connection for spiritual strength, you can easily be consumed by circumstance. Whether we are consciously aware or not, we all have a set of beliefs and principles by which we live. These core values influence our thoughts and emotions, and thus every important action we take.

The Benefits of Belief

Religious or spiritual belief in general has also been proven to have tremendous health benefits. Programs like Alcoholics Anonymous that have a spiritual component, despite one's particular faith, have been highly effective in recovery from drugs, alcohol, and various other addictions. Spirituality has also been linked to speedy recovery from surgery and maintenance of nominal blood pressure. Several studies also show that strong religious belief enables one to fare better with chronic illnesses ranging from heart disease to arthritis to cancer.

You cannot deny the results of spirituality, despite your personal interpretation. An article posted by the University of Maryland's Center of

Integrated Medicine notes that spirituality not only reduces stress but also promotes healing that has a significant impact on your immune, cardiovascular, hormonal, and nervous system.[15] The article goes on to cite significant research that more specifically links the spiritual qualities of faith, hope, forgiveness, love, and prayer to good health:

Faith - increases stress resistance [16]

Hope - reduces depression and other illness and extends lifespan

Forgiveness - reduces stress and anger and enhances emotional coping skills

Love - reduces stress and encourages health compliance

Prayer - improves overall health and reduces the likelihood of health complications

Figure 3-2

In relation to a life in the spotlight, spirituality is about stability. A life of fame is usually filled with dramatic change. You can be a hero today and a villain tomorrow. You can be an unknown today and a superstar tomorrow. So, if you don't have some constant to keep you grounded, you will lose control and be tossed around by every wind of change. **Before you become the center of attention, you should give attention to your center.** Covey suggests that the spiritual life based on principles is the most effective way to live, and that centering our lives on anything else is a flawed way of living that will lead to complications.[17] He goes on to point out 10 common centers and their flaws:

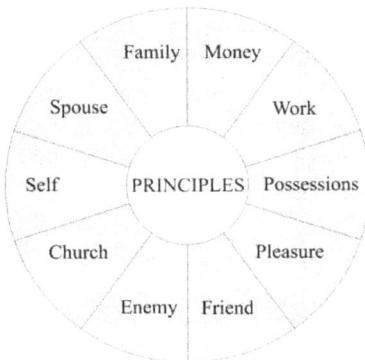

Figure 3-3. Life Centers. Adapted from *The 7 Habits of Highly Effective People: Restoring Character Ethic* (p.125), by S.R. Covey, 2004, New York, NY: Free Press. Copyright 2004 by S.R. Covey.

WHERE DO YOU LIVE?

Your Ideal Environment

When it comes to success, your environment is very important. Just as snow causes you to bundle up, and heat makes you shed layers, where and with whom you spend your time affects you inside and outside of the spotlight. A bad environment positions you for the opportunity to fail, while a good environment positions you for the opportunity to succeed. Note that I did not say that environment *causes* you to succeed or fail. An environment does not achieve or make mistakes. You do. In addition, environment can be relative. A bad environment for you may be a good environment for another.

Environment is a factor in every component of your identity. If you are in an environment where your spirit is strengthened, your physicality, mentality, emotionality, and sociality will likely line up with your spirit. However, in an environment where your spirit is broken, energy is zapped from all other faculties as well. Once you have discovered your identity, you will begin to see what environments give you the most opportunity. For example, by living in a city conducive to your endeavors, you have taken steps to alter your environment in a way such as to give yourself a better opportunity to succeed.

Positioning Yourself for Opportunity

Opportunity is about being in the right place at the right time, and that often requires you to leave an environment that does not have the opportunities you need. Opportunity is not something you wait for. Instead, you chase it; you seize it! You may need to surround yourself with different friends, live in a different part of the world, work at a different job, or communicate to a different audience to position yourself for an opportunity to succeed. And once you have that opportunity, your preparation or lack thereof will be exposed. **Preparation is all about your condition, but opportunity is all about your position**.

Never put yourself in a position where you cannot change your environment, even for a little while. **The spotlight is a place that you visit, not a place where you live**. In addition to having an environment away from fame, you should retreat away from everything occasionally to re-energize yourself. Every meeting, every performance, and every speech will draw on your identity, so take the time to refuel and replace what you lose.

Darkness Retreats

In his "Leadership Lifters" articles, pastor and author Rick Warren developed a slogan that reminds you to take a break from the business of life: "Divert Daily, Withdraw Weekly, and Abandon Annually."[19] But, to deal with the rigors of fame, I have inserted two more times for an extra boost of rejuvenation: Maintain Monthly and Quit Quarterly. Review each refreshment period and determine where you can implement them into your life.

> **Divert Daily:** Use that lunch break; don't work through it. Squeeze in a power nap. Pray or meditate. Take a moment for yourself each day.

> **Withdraw Weekly:** It's called a week-*end* for a reason. If you are going hard seven days a week, you will eventually crash. Put the work down for a day or two.

> **Maintain Monthly:** This is a great time to schedule your spa treatments, massages, and other monthly treats. Do something for yourself every month.

> **Quit Quarterly:** This is a good time for self-evaluation and self-reflection. It's a mini-break like the quarter breaks of a basketball game where you can take a minute and review the effectiveness of your game plan.

> **Abandon Annually:** Every year you should just leave. You might not even tell anyone where you are going. Get away from everything, leave your work at home, and enjoy a vacation. Even after a bad year, you still deserve it.

Sacred Spaces

You may also want to consider a sacred space in your home or the use of feng shui, an ancient Chinese system which creates positive energy in an indoor or outdoor environment. This design system is very popular, and it is used often during the conception of shopping centers and office buildings. For example, feng shui expert Katherine Anne Lewis, founder of Harmony and Balance, was consulted for the building of The Grove in Los Angeles, CA and the Americana at Brand in Glendale, CA.[20] And, you can apply the same principles in your home to create a place of stability amongst the instabilities of fame.

If you are still skeptical of the power of your space, just ask Reese Witherspoon, Madonna, Cindy Crawford or Courtney Love. They have all applied these methods under the direction of celebrity yoga guru Gurmukh

Kaur Khalsa.[21] Khalsa also recommends that your sacred space, at work or at home, should be wherever your eye is drawn.[22] Don't have objects in your home or office just to have them. Everything around you in your environment affects you whether you realize it or not.

Clean and Colorful Surroundings

Lastly, live clutter-free and really consider the colors and elements you surround yourself with along with their placement. It is amazing how cleanliness externally can affect cleanliness internally and vice versa. Try not to be junky. If there are loose odds and ends on the floor, on your desk, or under your bed, it reflects internal chaos and disorganization. It can be a sign that you are too busy, that you have been in the spotlight too long, and that you are neglecting yourself. Remember, "a cluttered room is a cluttered mind."

■□■

Hopefully you are beginning to see the complexity of the various components of your identity and the importance of clearly defining and maintaining yourself. The famous person who spins out of control seems so out of touch, but it should not surprise you. Any garden that is not properly maintained will inevitably grow wild.

Carefully monitor how you think, what you say, why you be, and where you live in order to keep a solid mental and spiritual focus. Fame is fun and games, but in between the parties, reality hits—and it hits hard! Learn from past celebrities regarding what mental illnesses you may be prone to and take steps to strengthen your mental fortitude. Speak positively about yourself to counter the negative elements that will come your way. Center your evolving life in the constant of spirituality, supplementing every other component of your identity with its many benefits. And, be aware of your environment. Know when to work, when to play, and when to rest. If you develop a strong foundation in your spirituality, mentality, and physicality, you can thrive in the social and emotional realms as well.

Works Cited

1 (Cronin)

2 ("50 Famous")

3 (Allen)

4 (People In Sports)

5 (Smith)

6,7 (Adams)

8 (Thorn)

9 (Borges)

10 (Jopson)

11,12 (Avalon)

13("Flash Facts")

14 (Petronzio)

15, 16 ("Spirituality")

17 (Covey 122)

18 (Covey 125)

19 (Warren)

20 (Lewis)

21, 22 (L. House and S. House 170)

4

CONNECTION AND DETECTION

The social and emotional components of identity are somewhat more refined qualities in comparison to the spiritual, mental, and physical basics. Also, social success and emotional stability tend to be similar in that they are usually about finding the middle ground and avoiding extremes. Your social and emotional behavior is quite exposed in the spotlight, so it is best to address any issues beforehand.

Socially, you should be aware of how you interact with others. You must be able to speak to people and make your point without regret. You will need to be careful of who you surround yourself with and be aware of current social issues and the accepted social practices in various environments.

You should be able to identify your emotions and find healthy ways to manage those emotions. This sounds simple, but we as human beings are so complex that social and emotional issues can be difficult to understand without a wealth of life experience and significant introspection.

SOCIAL SUCCESS

The way you deal with others is a huge component of people's perception of you, and your reputation in this regard can spread like wildfire, especially if the report is not favorable. Studies show that 95% of people share bad experiences.[1] Are you bossy, arrogant, and hard to work with? Are you friendly, compassionate, and easy-going? Where do you stand on the significant issues of the world, and what social contribution is expected of you? In the next few sections, we will examine five major social factors in a star's life: social skills, social support, social issues, social practices, and social responsibility.

Social Skills

If you are going to have a life in the spotlight, forget about being a total introvert or a recluse. You will constantly be surrounded by people, so you will need strong social skills to increase your comfort and success in social situations. Social skills are the skills that are necessary to communicate and interact with others.[2] These include verbal and non-verbal communications, and your ability to maneuver in the spotlight will correlate significantly with your social skills. **The road to the spotlight is paved with relationships, so before you travel on that road, it is your job to build it first**. You need to get in the habit now of starting and building beneficial relationships and ending other relationships that are detrimental to you. You may have to start a new road, extend an old road, repair a damaged road, or just bring out a jackhammer and tear a road down. Either way, the more efficient roads you have, the more likely you are to travel down one that takes you to fame.

    Your gateway to the next level isn't a door, it's a person. Stop looking for the door, and start looking for the individual(s) with the power to grant you access. And when you find these people, be prepared to interact with them confidently and naturally. Fame puts you in various social situations, and you should be knowledgeable and flexible enough to adjust your behavior in these social settings. To be socially successful in the spotlight, you need to be able to observe others critically to pick up on important social clues, interpret those clues, and form a response, often instantaneously. However, if you are more of an introvert like me, don't be discouraged. Social skills incorporate many behaviors which can be learned and developed. Some people are naturally charismatic, but if that is not you, do not fall victim to the myth that you cannot be as socially successful. For example, the person who is always the life of the party may not be the best listener, a skill more commonly associated with introverts. Assess yourself truthfully and find areas where you can improve yourself socially. Remember, it is all about relationship, and you never know who will hold the key to your success.

Straight Talk

Being in the spotlight draws people who want to use your position to further their own agendas, whether it lines up with yours or not. And, we often cater to others to a fault because we don't want to look like a mean person. However, being socially successful is not about getting people to like you; leave that to marketing and public relations! Let those components of your career fit you, not the other way around. If you are too concerned about getting people to like you, then you will do whatever it takes to accomplish that, even if it violates your core principles.

    Don't be a puppet for other people's opinions. The individuals who have had the most influence in history have had their own words, their own thoughts, and their own beliefs. Say what you say because you believe it, not because someone told you to say it.

Any kind of people-pleasing issues need to be worked out before you step into the spotlight. If they are not, you are sure to run into some major problems. Just ask Vanilla Ice. In interviews, the rapper admits that his hood hip hop persona was a fabrication by the industry.[3] Actress Anne Hathaway also has opened up about failed romantic relationships due to a people-pleasing mentality.[4] Mandy Moore has spoken about her bad habit of trying too much to get people to like her.[5] And, Jocelyn Wildenstein also known as "Catwoman," has spent over 4 million dollars to "fix" herself with plastic surgery after finding out that her husband was having an affair.[6] You can easily spin out of control and act out of character by submitting to the demand of others. Be confident in yourself, and let the true you speak.

Socializing Secrets

You may be in the spotlight because of what you can do, not what you say, so you might not be the best communicator. Believe it or not, this may be a problem that needs to be addressed immediately, and it is something I have struggled with as well. Being in the spotlight gives you a platform, and when you are on a platform, people want to hear what you have to say. Everyone knew me as a musician and would love to hear me play, but I would never say much. It would frustrate them because they would want to understand me, but as long as my mouth was shut, they could not. I would rarely talk because I was shy, I had trouble gathering my thoughts, I was battling depression, and I also stuttered. So, I began working on being a better communicator, and after years of struggle, I can attribute my growth to two important lessons.

The first lesson I learned was that repetition is the enemy of nervousness. Do what scares you, and then do it again and again. Every time you do it, you will be less afraid. Believe it or not, it's as simple as that. I began to take positions that forced me to talk to people from all walks of life. I worked backstage at a theater and had to interact with celebrities. I started a student organization on campus and had to speak confidently with group members and faculty. I led bands and singers with some of the most interesting personalities you have ever seen. I took marketing jobs that forced me to interact and talk with people. I put together a national educational tour where I not only played for but also talked to students in a lecture setting. People want to hear you speak, and when you do, it elevates you and adds an entirely new dimension to your persona. **Your abilities can make you an icon, but your words can make you an influence. Your abilities will cause people to notice you, but your words will cause people to follow you**.

I learned the second lesson in a roundabout way, but when I began to use it, it blew my mind. The secret of talking to people is asking questions.

Part of my issue was that I didn't know what to say to people, but when you ask questions, especially of genuine interest, the conversation just flows. This works because at the end of the day, we are all naturally self-centered, and we like to talk about ourselves. So, answering questions about ourselves gives us the perfect opportunity to do so.

Consider the role of Facebook and Twitter, currently the top two social media platforms. The writing is on the wall...literally. We live in an age where we can view the social lives of billions of people, and most status updates are a cry for attention: Look at how cool I am. Look at how smart I am. Look at what I did. I went to a hot party last night. I am so beautiful. I am friends with important people. This is our social networking. If you want to start a dialogue, ask a question, and then let the other person brag. Learn about them, and they just might want to learn about you as well.

Are you uncomfortable with speaking to people? If your answer is yes, then check out these 10 speech tips below.

1. Keep the "ums," "uhs," and "likes" to a minimum. They make you sound dumb.
2. Don't mumble. Project. This displays confidence and authority.
3. Be yourself. Don't be a faker. People like real.
4. Don't eat anything crazy before speaking...seriously.
5. Practice in the mirror. Your face should match your words.
6. Use your hands to communicate.
7. Move around when you talk. You're not a statue.
8. Record yourself. How does your voice sound? Shaky and nervous? Dull and boring?
9. XYZ – eXamine Your Zipper
10. Breath mints. Don't leave home without them.

Figure 4-1

Social Support

Social support, whether it be through family, friends, or colleagues is critical to social health in general, but even more critical for someone in the spotlight. When you start to drift off into the perils of star life, the people closest to you will hopefully give you perspective and keep you grounded. The hardest part, however, is determining their motives. And, when you become famous, those people tend to fall into one of two categories; I call them crutches and leeches.

Crutches vs. Leeches

Crutches are people who strengthen and support you. Leeches are people who drain you and use you to support themselves. It can be very difficult to distinguish between the two, and usually the only way to tell the difference is during a tough time. You don't know how good a crutch is until you twist your ankle. That's when your crutches show up. And, you can't tell if you have a leech until there's nothing more they can get from you. That's when your leeches leave you high and dry.

Discerning between a crutch and a leech, however, is not impossible. It requires what I call **social motive sensitivity: the ability to discern the disposition of others in a social setting**. I view this as a spiritual concept that goes back to the last chapter, and hopefully you are seeing that each component of your identity affects the other, whether negative or positive. To develop social motive sensitivity, you must be able to see a person not only with your eyes, but with you spirit. Sometimes I refer to it as "feeling" a person. Other people refer to it as getting a "vibe" from a person.

Recognizing Energy

We all give off energy, and I believe that if you are spiritually in tune, you can sense another's energy and gather some valuable information. We often use this in romantic relationships when we connect with someone. For example, with past girlfriends I could feel when something was wrong, and I would pry until they finally opened up and admitted. In a different scenario, I had a bad feeling about a promoter in Hollywood, but I ignored that feeling. He still owes me money today! The people who surround you will be extremely influential in your life, so determine if they are crutches or leeches before a bad situation occurs in which you will need them.

Social Issues

Social Issues In The Spotlight

Knowledge of social issues widens the number of people with whom you can relate. It also enables you to formulate your own concrete opinions and philosophies that you can live by and share. Again, when you are in the spotlight, people will want to hear what you have to say. They expect you to be knowledgeable not only about your particular area of expertise but also about various other subjects. Where do you stand on abortion? Do you believe in global warming? How can we end poverty? The topics don't even have to be that serious. It could come down to the hottest television show or the best sports team right now. If they are topics that many people care about, you should find out at least a little about it so that you can stay relevant, even if it isn't your cup of tea. When you are in the spotlight, people will expect you to have a solidified opinion on these kinds of issues, whether it relates to why you are in the spotlight or not. If you don't have an answer, you run the risk of looking foolish and uneducated, and people will turn away from you, even when they have no answers themselves.

Social Issues In The Darkness

Staying abreast of social issues is also a great tool for life balance. The life of fame can easily become a bubble that eventually alienates you from your fans, but social issues can take you out of the spotlight for a moment and increase your awareness of the world around you. For musicians who may spend days in the recording studio or for actors who can easily log 15-hour days on a movie set, it can be easy to sink into a miniature world for weeks or months at a time. However, by learning about others, you can remove the focus from yourself, acknowledge your place as just another human being in the global community, and gain various perspectives that will help you long-term.

Ways To Stay Informed

As you go through life in the spotlight, you will begin to notice that things can get pretty hectic. So, it will be difficult for you to find time to stay abreast of current events. In this case, technology and multi-tasking will be your best friends. News programs on television are partially entertainment, and the fluff which is a part of these shows will take up too much of your time. Instead, consider getting streaming updates to your phone or personal computer, so that you can quickly get the stories you want with facts you can use. You can also benefit by just keeping your eye on the newsfeeds of your social media outlets. In terms of multitasking, I'm a big fan of car radio. I rarely listen to music when I'm driving, and instead, I multitask with talk radio news programming. Every time I get into my car, I don't just waste time in traffic, I learn something new. The gym is another great place to multitask, and I see many businessmen do this every day. Increase your body *and* your mind while on the cardio machines by flipping through an industry magazine or other relevant periodical, or watching a news program. You can also take a more hands-on approach to increasing your awareness of social issues by doing a bit of traveling. Your trip could be around the block or across the border. Either way, you can increase your awareness if you make an effort. Lastly, holding a position in which you teach or mentor the younger generation can be very valuable. Kids and younger adults will be more into current events and popular culture. And, they will be glad to share their new fads with you.

Social Practices

Going With The Flow

Social practices refer to accepted behaviors, customs, traditions, and more. An understanding of these practices will make you less likely to offend others or embarrass yourself, as being in the spotlight increases the number of diverse situations you encounter and the people with whom you interact. For example, knowing which fork is the salad fork, not wearing certain colors in the hood, choosing acceptable attire for a formal event, and removing shoes in an Asian household are all social behaviors that I have had to learn because of my talents connecting me with so many different people. And, if you do not prepare, your underdevelopment during common settings like interviews and social functions will be exposed. Knowledge only of yourself and what you do will make you feel painfully out of place and socially awkward when interacting with others, so make it a point to learn the social practices of your surrounding community.

Swimming Upstream

Understanding accepted social practices can also prepare you for the backlash and consequences of going against the status quo. For instance, if you are against gay marriage, it would be good to know that millions of people support it and will disagree with you. The clearer the picture you have about both sides, the less likely you are to put your foot in your mouth and alienate others. You should ponder several social issue questions before you act. What is the social climate like right now regarding this topic? What are the main arguments on each side? What language would allow people to see your point of view in a non-offensive way?

Still, remember that it is OK to go against the way things are now. That is how change occurs. The people who went against the grain are the people we read about in history books, and many who are famous now were hated and misunderstood during their time of achievement. **You can permutate social practices, but there is a price for being a pioneer**.

Social Responsibility

Social responsibility, your obligation to society, is a highly-debated topic when it comes to people in the spotlight. Many feel that those who have much visibility and influence are obligated to contribute to society, not only in a positive way, but also in an expanded role. Others believe that stars are still just human beings who should be entitled to normal lives and not held to unrealistic standards and obligations. However, I side more with the former argument.

The Case For Social Responsibility

Celebrity status is at its core an elevation, a promotion, not in terms of being better than another or sometimes not even in terms of achievement, but in terms of visibility and influence. With that in mind, a heightened social responsibility is part of the deal. If you receive a promotion at your job, you usually are paid more, but it also requires you to do more and/or take on more responsibility. It is the same way with celebrity status. There is responsibility attached to that level of influence.

The Outer-Inner Connection

Social responsibility also goes back to identity. What you do reflects who you are. So, who are you? Are you selfish, or do you genuinely care about others? Your level of social responsibility is another communication tool that people will use to understand and evaluate you on an ethical and moral level, and for some, a spiritual level. The totality of you as a person, not just the talent you possess, is in the spotlight. So, **the magnification of your life requires the magnification of your efforts**. If you have been given more, more will be required of you. And, if you choose not to meet those requirements, you will be given less and/or what you have will be reduced. If this sounds overwhelming, know that social responsibility does not always have to be active. It can also be passive. Instead of always trying to do something positive, you can refrain from negative societal actions and still promote social responsibility.

The Role Model Debate

On the other hand, there is a misconception that being a role model means living a perfect life with no mistakes. However, that mentality is erroneous, and you should not put that kind of pressure on yourself. The role model label should not be a sign of perfection because perfection in humanity is impossible. Still, it's OK to be a role model and have people consider you as such. Just know and encourage your supporters to remember that **being a role model isn't always about doing the right thing all the time. Sometimes, it's about doing the right thing after you've done the wrong thing**.

The Cycle of Giving

Social responsibility also fuels the economy of your celebrity by enabling a balance between your ability and your community. When you give worthy entertainment, knowledge, or leadership, the community in turn gives you time, attention, money, praise, etc. This cycle of giving between your efforts and your environment is a process that is fundamental to keeping you in the spotlight.

Now, this transaction has its place, but this level of giving is commercial and mechanical. Giving back deeper, more fundamental societal contributions, however, strengthens the community that enables your celebrity. How can someone buy your music if they can't buy food? Are you training future leaders or just acquiring followers?

People increase your ability to be a celebrity. In turn, you should increase the people's ability to be supporters. **When you give of your talent, you elate the people; when you give of yourself, you elevate the people**. The problem with just giving your talent is that your talents get old. Your positive social impact, however, does not. People might say, "I'm tired of his comedy." But, they are less likely to say, "I'm tired of him helping me and improving my life."

EMOTIONAL SUCCESS

Emotional health is such an appropriate ending to the five components of identity because it relies so much on the physical, mental, spiritual, and social and shows how they all integrate. Emotional health is incredibly important because life in the spotlight is often a roller coaster that takes your emotions along for the ride. Take a moment and really think about how you handle things emotionally. Or better yet, ask someone else to evaluate you. Are you ready for a hundred people telling you how much you suck? Are you ready for thousands who "love" you? What about the tens of thousands who absolutely hate you? How about the stalker who wants to harm you and your family? When your personal failures, your business flops, your dirty laundry, and your bad relationships are all exposed to the world, how will you really handle that?

Think of your highest high and your lowest low. Now, if you increase those feelings exponentially, that is what they will feel like when you are famous. If you are not careful, those emotions can easily get out of hand, turning you into a loopy space cadet, a tense ball of anger, or a suicidal recluse. And don't say, "It would never happen to me." That would be your first mistake. The intensity of fame will require a detailed introspective look at your emotions. If you constantly fly off the handle, your fans and friends will turn away. Instead, you will need to control your emotions and not allow them to control you.

Identifying Your Emotions

Before you can manage your emotions, you must identify them. And, to clearly identify your emotions, you have to go deeper than "I feel bad," or "I feel good." You need to be more descriptive and the Feeling Wheel developed by Dr. Gloria Wilcox is a great starting point for more clearly defining the breadth and depth of your emotions. The wheel starts with six basic emotions at its core, and then expands outward, listing more possible underlying emotions related to the core emotion. For example, if you say that you are sad, I can only guess wildly at what will help you manage that emotion. I could buy you a gift, and you may still be sad because a gift may not be the answer for you. However, if you use the feeling wheel and say that you are sad because you are lonely, and you are lonely because you feel isolated, then

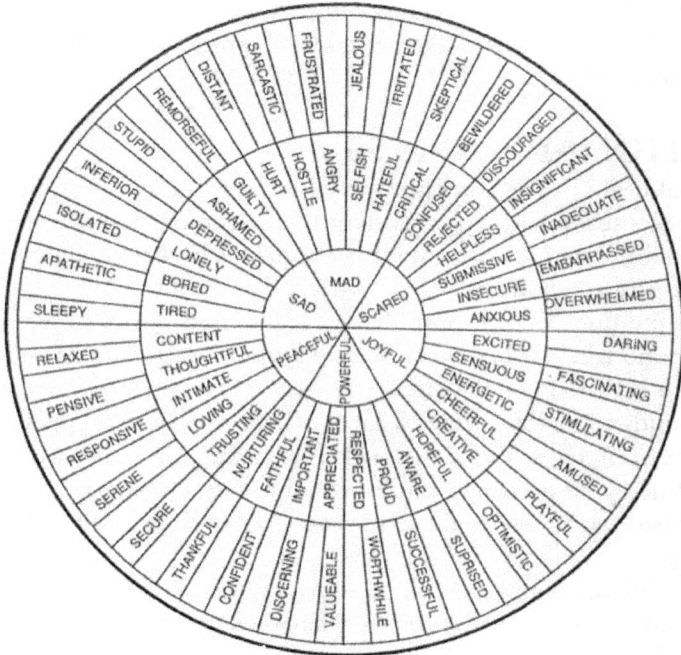

Figure 4-2. The Feeling Wheel. Reprinted from *Feelings: Converting Negatives to Positives*, by Dr. G. Wilcox, 2001, Morris Publishing. Copyright 2001 by Dr. Gloria Wilcox.

you have more clearly defined your sadness with some other descriptive underlying feelings. With this knowledge, I would spend more time with you instead of buying gifts. Identifying emotions with this kind of specificity will help you greatly in management.

Take time out and tune in to your emotions. **Identify what makes you tick and what ticks you off**. Think of the range of emotions you experience every day. What internal forces (self-esteem, internal thoughts, physical wellness, etc.) cause feelings for you? What external forces (people, words, circumstances, environments, etc.) affect your feelings? What feelings are most dominant in you? What feelings do you act on? What feelings do you subdue? This is all part of knowing yourself, and when you know yourself, you can manage your emotions.

Don't ever succumb to the if-it-feels-good-then-do-it mentality. That is a life controlled by emotions. Remember, success in the spotlight is about building structure. But, emotions are volatile, despite being completely healthy and necessary expressions. They are not the layers of the cake; they are more like the icing on top. If you give emotions a foundational role, then you will live in instability, and your unstable structure will likely collapse.

Managing Your Emotions

Once you have identified your emotions, you can begin managing them in healthy ways. Healthy emotional management is about not letting your emotions alone dictate how you think and behave. And like many of the other identity components, emotional management is about avoiding the extremes in which your emotions become harmful. Management, however, is not the non-expression or ignorance of emotion. Bottling up your emotions will eventually cause you to explode, releasing stored feelings at once, quite possibly in a misdirected manner.

Emotional management is also not about being happy all the time. Being generally happy and content is quite possible, but being happy all the time with a perfect life is a fantasy. Success doesn't automatically equal constant happiness. In fact, scientific studies are now proving that it is the other way around, and people who are just generally happy tend to be more successful.[8] We are too complex to be happy all the time in this unstable life. Don't be fooled by other people in the spotlight who seem to have a perfect lifestyle. The same star who seems on top of the world is too often the star with the most troubles.

To manage your emotions, you want to first start with all the other components of your life:

> **Examine your physical health:** Proper diet and exercise that balances work, rest, and play; access to sunlight; flattering clothes and accessories; the avoidance of drugs and alcohol; and pretty much anything else that improves you physically will also improve your

emotional health.

Examine your mental health: Learning new things, managing stress, controlling negative thoughts, and limiting worry all improve your emotional health.

Examine your spiritual health: A purpose or meaning in life, contentment with life, a zest for living, devotion to spiritual or religious beliefs, meditation, prayer, and a good environment will improve your emotional health.

Examine your social health: Social support systems and positive relationships, self-esteem, community impact, and achievement all improve your emotional health.

Beyond these core elements, emotional management is just a matter of allowing for logic to influence your decisions and considering the consequences of the behaviors your emotions may arouse. All topics previously covered lay the groundwork for a successful life in the spotlight, but emotional health is a significant issue that you definitely want to get a handle on particularly before you are involved with the media. Reporters will do everything they can to push your buttons because an emotional wreck is a great story for them. So, be mindful of your emotional responses. You will have a hard-enough time trying to keep people away from the other personal facets of your life.

■□■□

Social and emotional strength are valuable because they are the link between your core and your crowd. They are the first elements that specifically focus on your interaction with others, hopefully sparking enough interest to initiate and grow your fame. Those who are successful in the spotlight tend to have a level of social skill and emotional management that enables that success. For some, these abilities just come naturally. Others, however, may really have to work on social integration and emotional management. Additionally, you should seek out the opinions and insights of other people in these matters, because your actions from the perspective of your audience may be interpreted in a totally different way. However, with a clear view of yourself socially and emotionally along with the other components of your identity, you can not only understand how others view you, but also control what you want to be seen. This separates your private life from your public life, and in doing so, you can present a more finished product to the masses. In the next chapter, you will see how all the pieces come together with the glue of structure and management in final preparation for the successful launch into fame.

Works Cited

1 (Dimensional Research 2)

2 ("Social Skills")

3 ("Vanilla Ice")

4 ("Anne Hathaway")

5 ("ADVICEFORLIVING")

6 ("Bride Of Wildenstein")

7 (Wilcox)

8 ("Review Of Research")

5
BUILT
FOR
FAME

Now that we have covered the main components of identity, it is important to understand how to order and balance each attribute in a structured way that will sustain you during fame. If you want to be famous, and you're starting from ground zero, where do you begin? What external components are necessary? And, how does each successive component relate to one another? How do people use or misuse their identity in the quest for fame? Knowing what pieces are necessary is just the first step; you must also know how to put the puzzle together.

THE TOSS THEORY

In my search for the answers to these types of questions regarding the basic organization of our lives, I was immediately inclined to review Maslow's Hierarchy of Needs. Abraham Maslow was a 20th century American psychologist who is best known for developing a building-block theory regarding the order of the essential needs of man. The hierarchy starts off with the most basic needs, and when those needs are met, one moves to more high-level needs. As you can see in Figure 5-1, Maslow starts with physiological needs. These include necessities like food, water, and air. They are basic needs that we cannot survive without. The hierarchy then progresses to needs of safety, love and belonging, esteem, and finally self-actualization.

Now in relation to the topics covered in this book, I began to see a correlation between Maslow's Hierarchy of Needs and most of the components needed for a structured life of fame. Maslow's physiological level relates obviously to our physical topic. I saw the safety tier as a relation to finances and other resources that will be discussed later. The level of love and belonging relates to our topic of social connection. Esteem mirrors our emotional discussion, and self-actualization identifies with the mental-spiritual element and our gifts to the world.

MASLOW'S
HIERARCHY
★ OF NEEDS ★

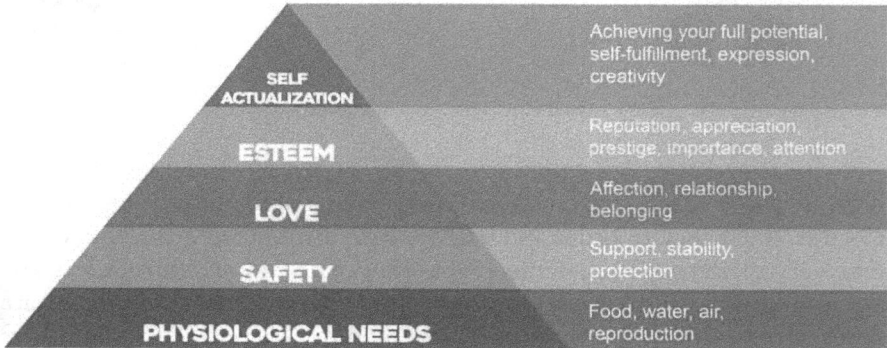

SELF ACTUALIZATION	Achieving your full potential, self-fulfillment, expression, creativity
ESTEEM	Reputation, appreciation, prestige, importance, attention
LOVE	Affection, relationship, belonging
SAFETY	Support, stability, protection
PHYSIOLOGICAL NEEDS	Food, water, air, reproduction

Figure 5-1

I slowly began to see that the facets of identity are more than a circle that completes us; they are also a stairway of sequential steps that can be organized for successful fame.

With a continued focus on the life of fame and the use of Maslow's Hierarchy of Needs as a reference, I eventually came up with the tree of stable stardom theory, or the toss theory. If you look at Figure 5-2, you will see that the theory conveniently aligns with the actual parts of a tree, from roots to fruits. In addition to the tree categories and/or subcategories, each section also has an associated action verb. This natural example will greatly help you understand the structure of the ideal stable star life.

Roots of Regulation

The base of the toss theory starts with the roots, and I call these the roots of regulation. Notice also that the roots are divided. Just like a tree, there are roots below ground that you cannot see and roots above ground which are visible. I believe the roots below ground and the basis for any stable life of fame are spiritual. Spirituality gives a singular focus, a moral compass, a direction in life that provides tremendous stability when held to steadfastly. As we saw earlier, spirituality operates outside of the natural world. So, when the natural world changes—as it frequently does—your spiritual connection to something beyond it can remain anchored.

TREE OF STABLE
STARDOM
★ THEORY ★

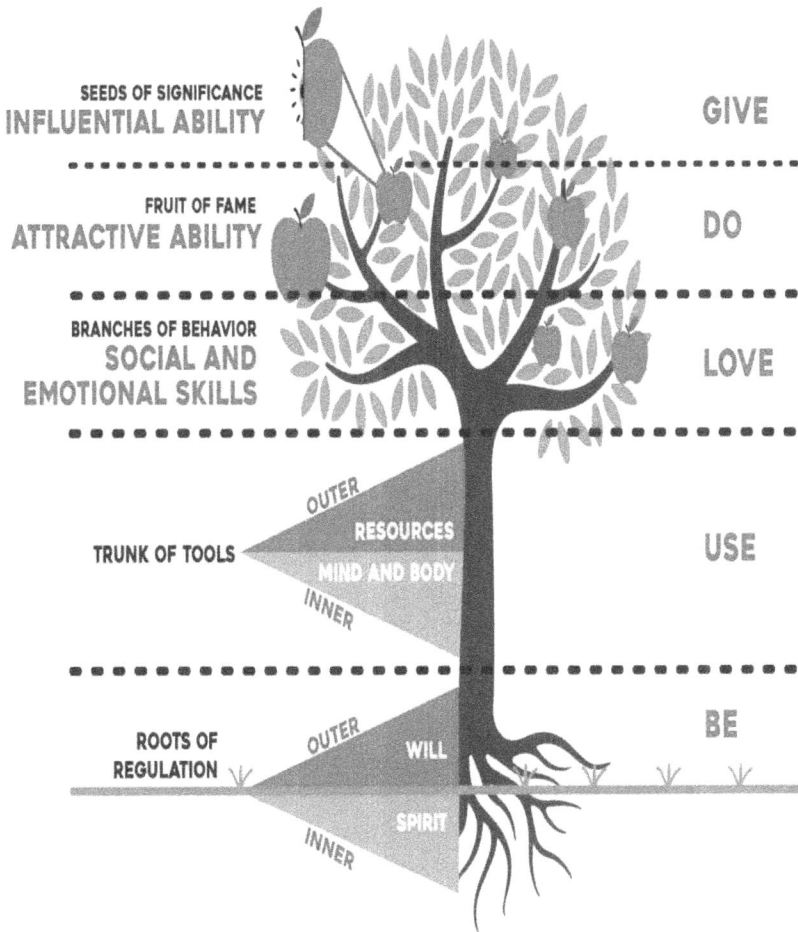

SEEDS OF SIGNIFICANCE INFLUENTIAL ABILITY		GIVE
FRUIT OF FAME ATTRACTIVE ABILITY		DO
BRANCHES OF BEHAVIOR SOCIAL AND EMOTIONAL SKILLS		LOVE
TRUNK OF TOOLS	OUTER RESOURCES MIND AND BODY INNER	USE
ROOTS OF REGULATION	OUTER WILL SPIRIT INNER	BE

Figure 5-2

Your will is also listed as a root of regulation because it is the outward representation of the spiritual root. It is the projection of your core into the natural world for everyone to see. Now, if your tree is healthy, the transition between the roots below and above should be seamless. In fact, every part of your tree should be reflective of and traceable to your roots. They truly are extremely important to your success.

Before the drugs, sex scandals, and bankruptcy, a famous person's problems most likely begin with a weakness in their roots. A weak core makes you vulnerable, and you must be strong in a life of fame to survive. For example, a casting director promises you a role in the next big movie if you sleep with him tonight. In a moment like that, your core is immediately tested. That outward decision will be the projection of an inner value. Either you are willing to sacrifice your body for fame (And it isn't just this one time; you will do it again). Or at your core, you believe that giving up your body for sex to obtain a movie role is wrong. The choice and the consequences are up to you, but the real problems occur when your will and beliefs contradict each other. That signifies internal conflict and confusion, which are recipes for disaster.

When the spirit says, "yes," the will should reflect, "yes." When the spirit says, "no," the will should reflect, "no." But when the spirit says, "yes," and the will reflects, "no" or vice versa, that means that you have allowed something or someone to come in between the inward and outward manifestation of your very being. And again, that is dangerous territory. That is when you become a puppet for others. You need regulation. And that starts in the roots.

Trunk of Tools

The next part of the tree of stable stardom is the trunk of tools. Once you have established your core, your essence, you then need to be properly equipped to work in fame. Just like the roots of regulation, there are two parts to the trunk, the inner trunk which is your body and the outer trunk which is external resources. Your body is your most valuable tool, and without a healthy body, you cannot function at optimum levels. Your body is the engine in the car of your fame. The rims, tinted windows, and sound system may be nice, but if the car won't start because your engine is bad, it really defeats the primary purpose of the car as a means of transportation. An attractive, well-kept body will only enhance your stardom in our visual age, so make it a priority.

The outer trunk symbolizes the other resources outside of your physical being. And, I use the term resources very broadly to describe several things that can help and/or protect you on your journey. A reliable car that can take you to all your appointments is a resource. A quality education is a resource. A supporting side job, a life insurance policy, a business plan, and health care are all resources.

Now each of the aforementioned resources is different, but there is one common thread that runs through them all. Money. When you talk about resources, there is usually some sort of financial element; however, the attainment of a resource does not always require that you pay for it. Still, on the road to fame, you most likely will be at a leveraging disadvantage at some point and require financing. And for many talented people, that financing is the great divide between obscurity and a skyrocketed career. The importance of money cannot be underestimated. Money is so effective that just having large amounts of it alone exponentially increases your potential for fame. Even so, the purchase of a resource with your money is just one of the many avenues by which you may obtain that resource.

You will need to review your body and resources frequently because they have a nasty habit of dwindling away. It can be so easy to pack on a few pounds, ignore a physical defect, or neglect your need for a better car or more education. And, you will be incredibly frustrated when your number is called for 15 minutes of fame, but you do not have the tools to be your best or even answer the call at all. If the world is looking for a screwdriver, but all you have is hammers, you will be passed over. Instead, the next person who has prepared himself by investing in screwdrivers will be taking your spotlight.

Branches of Behavior

Next in the tree of stable stardom are the branches of behavior, which deal with your emotional and social connections. Here, branches are the perfect analogy as this stage consists of connecting with yourself and others. This is similar to the manner in which tree branches extend, connect, and intertwine. The branches mark a significant midway point in the tree at which you transition from dealing more with yourself to dealing more with the audience that makes you famous.

All of these stages are important, but I urge you to take your development on the social and emotional level very seriously. Missteps in the branches of behavior can literally make or break your career. If the branch breaks off, no fruit can grow. This is the part where a serious endeavor can turn into a three-ring circus. You absolutely must have a handle on these two areas or they will surely sabotage your career.

Our social and emotional facets really highlight our complexity as human beings, and the human elements of your career, good or bad, make great stories. However, a great story might not be so great for you if it is snatched up by the media. How many times have you seen a star in the media spiral out of control because of a social or emotional issue? The number of potentially devastating scenarios seems almost endless. An impromptu rant ticks off a few people and turns your fan base against you. Your song lyrics are banned from the radio. You get into a fight because you can't control your anger. Your girlfriend or boyfriend dumps you in a national embarrassment. Depression takes over you at a low point in your career. The list can go on and on. I know that it can be hard sometimes to see what your social and emotional health have to do with you being famous, but don't take your behavior lightly. Remember, the branches of behavior are a pivotal point in the tree where you move from just developing yourself to putting that developed self out in front of others and developing relationships.

Fruit of Fame

The next section of the tree is the fruit of fame. Ideally, this is where your talent meets your tree; where your stability couples with your ability to draw attention. Just as a natural tree produces fruit, your tree of stable stardom should produce the fruit of fame. Here, we use the action verb "do." What do you do? What do you offer? What makes you stand out from the rest? Why are you elevated above another? This section is all about what you bring to the table.

Now remember, who you are and what you do are certainly corollary but definitely different. And hopefully the classification and particularly the action verbs in the toss theory enable you to visualize that more clearly. However, people from the outside looking in will tend to group you into categories because they have no personal day-to-day relationship with you. It is easy for us to process others in general terms: the athlete, the jokester, the prima donna. If the roots of regulation, the trunk of tools, and the branches of behavior were the book on you, the fruit of fame would be Cliffs Notes.

Understanding what your fame is and how it is perceived will enable you to use it more effectively to accomplish your goals. This understanding of fame is important for two reasons. First, from your perspective, you don't want to turn your job into your identity. Fame is extremely volatile and should never be a basis for true identity or self-worth. The second reason comes from the perspective of your audience. There is an interesting verse in the Bible in which Jesus says, "By their fruit, you will recognize them."[2] People who are close to you may see the various components of your tree firsthand, but the masses will only know you by your fruit. They will only know you by what you do. Their understanding of you will be a general conclusion drawn from the fruit that they see. With that in mind, it will be imperative for you to understand the qualities of fame discussed in Chapter 6 so that you may use that knowledge to produce the most desirable fruit that you possibly can.

Seeds of Significance

For many people, their tree of stable stardom stops at fame. And who can blame them? That's the goal, to be famous, right? Well, it is *a* goal; however, there is another level that is so incredible that it completely dwarfs the fruit of fame. That next level is the seeds of significance. Fame is really a selfish endeavor, but the seeds of significance are all about being unselfish and giving to other people.

In nature, a single tree can produce millions, possibly billions of seeds, and you can literally start a forest with just one tree. Likewise, the seeds of significance are the key to an exponential growth factor that goes far beyond you individually. They are literally little reproductions of yourself, and people who identify with and are influenced by your tree will integrate your seed into their own tree. This is the leap from many people knowing who you are to starting a movement, a new philosophy, a culture exponentially larger than you can ever be as just a well-known individual. The seeds of significance are about influencing the lives of those around you and possibly the lives of those to come.

We have even created nomenclature to identify where seeds of significance have been sown. Lady Gaga has her Little Monsters. Justin Bieber has his Beliebers. *Star Trek* has Trekkies. Even the word Christian is translated little Christ. Another excellent example occurs in social media. Notice how Myspace and Facebook allow you to connect with "friends." You could compare this to the social branches of behavior. However, Twitter and Instagram allow you to connect with "followers," which is more comparable to the seeds of significance. Twitter operates in a totally different manner than the other social media tools, and you could even argue that Twitter is more of an influential medium than a social medium. The people who make a difference are the ones who significantly impact the lives of others. **Don't just accumulate friends, gather followers**.

Implementing the TOSS Theory

Please understand that the toss theory is a perfect world scenario to be implemented in an imperfect world by imperfect people. It would be nice if we could develop and master each stage before moving onto the next, yet the imperfections in ourselves and the world around us are the blessings that allow us to be unique individuals and the curses that prevent us from flawlessly implementing such life structures. There may be some hang-ups in your life that you may never get over. You may never look physically "ideal." Or, you may always be a bit socially awkward. Don't let that stop you from moving on and developing other areas of your life. The tree is a linear building-block example for organization and understanding, but in reality, the toss theory can be more like keeping a series of spinning plates twirling in the air. You will constantly have to revisit sections of your tree as you grow and evolve.

You can even compare the growth tools of plants with your own. For instance, plants require sunlight for energy. Similarly, for growth, you need to draw energy from various sources in order to work and accomplish. Plants also need water for nutrients, and you will also need to channel the nutrients drawn in from your roots into all the other components of your tree, creating a stream of consistency. Thirdly, plants also engage in the process of respiration just like animals and humans, and this creates an exchange of oxygen and carbon dioxide. You should mimic this respiration process and seek to create exchanges in your life. Once you are in an atmosphere that is conducive for growth, you should determine what you can "give off" to the world in order to get something back.

I also cannot emphasize enough the value of the appropriate usage of the correlating action verbs within the tree. Inappropriate use of a section can be just as harmful as neglecting it, and this is most likely the number one cause of instability and eventual downfall in the lives of the famous. The wrong verb can poison your efforts, so be cognizant of your actions. Doing the right thing the wrong way can make you infamous instead of famous.

Just imagine all the ways you can cause problems for yourself by switching some of the associated verbs. We have already discussed that what you do and who you are (the *be* verb) are two different things. If your identity lies in what you do, when you can no longer do that, it will be the beginning of an unnecessary identity crisis. It is also very common to love resources (usually money) or love the body (usually sexually). However, they are tools you should use, not things you should love. Contrarily, in the branches of behavior we often use people instead of loving them. This is a cold-hearted approach to fame that will produce bad fruit and animosity toward you. We can also give the fruit of fame instead of giving the seeds of significance. That sounds noble in comparison to the other examples, but once your fruit is gone, that's it. Giving the fruit is the sure road to a very quick 15 minutes of fame. If you want longevity, you must give seeds not fruit.

I believe the application of this theory will not only increase the quality of your life but also increase your chances for fame and more importantly significance. With proper usage, the toss theory can provide a stable structure that will strengthen and sustain you during the whirlwind that is fame. The concept is simple, but the application can be challenging. Even I am far from mastering it…and I came up with it! It will take a great deal of discipline and dedication to live such a balanced life. Even so, the awareness of these components and their order, and the attempt to grow and improve in each area will immediately separate you from the pack. That separation is the fundamental essence of fame.

PERSONAL MANAGEMENT

Success in structured stardom is highly influenced by your ability to manage yourself and manage other people. Unfortunately, the first is hard to do, and the second is even harder. How many promises have you made to yourself that were soon broken? How many New Year's resolutions have fallen apart by February? And have you ever tried to get a group of people to all do the same thing? It's nearly impossible. Despite these difficulties; however, you can still be an effective manager of yourself and others by understanding and properly using time and motivation. **Good timing will produce efficiency, and good motivation will produce effort**. You don't just become a star and sustain that stardom by accident. There is strategy involved, and the consistent management of self and others with the understanding of timing and motivating factors will help you put all the pieces together without becoming overwhelmed.

The way you live is very telling of your self-management, and the way you spend your time usually falls into one of four categories described by Covey: pressure, popularity, pleasure or priority. If you are acting on pressure, you are in an emergency situation. You may be blindsided by an ordeal or suffering the consequences of a lack of planning. If you are acting on popularity, you are engaged in something at the request of someone else. You may be working on one matter when someone interrupts with another issue, taking away your attention. Or, maybe you are doing something just to fit in or get people to notice you. If you are acting on pleasure, you are just trying to relax or have fun. You could be reading a book, watching a movie, playing video games, or hanging out with friends. And lastly, if you are acting on priority, you are working on objectives connected to a predetermined goal. You may be planning for your career, studying for a class, budgeting your money, or working on any other part of your tree of stable stardom. Consider a day of your life, or better yet, a week and identify how much time you spend in each area.

None of the personal management sections are bad; however, spending an inappropriate amount of time in any one place is not good. Although priority is obviously the noblest category, you cannot spend your whole life there. You need to experience pressure, popularity, and pleasure for life balance. The amount of time you spend in each section can also vary greatly

	Urgent	Not Urgent
Important	Pressure	Priority
Not Important	Popularity	Pleasure

Figure 5-3. Time Management Quadrants. Adapted from *The 7 Habits of Highly Effective People: Restoring Character Ethic* (p.151), by S.R. Covey, 2004, New York, NY: Free Press. Copyright 2004 by S.R. Covey.

depending on your personality, your beliefs, your circumstances, your goals, and more. However, I do recommend some general rules of thumb for anyone in the spotlight. First, although the largest portion of your time should be spent on priority, all your time should not be spent there. This will ensure a dedication and investment to accomplishing the goals you have set forth and a prevention of crisis that will turn emergency situations into occasional events. With that in mind, the next rule of thumb is that pressure situations, especially those you can prevent, should be reduced at all costs. Too much pressure will stress you out and distract you from your goals.

Lastly, you should be able to define each category in a way that accounts for your fame goals and does not confuse your time management efforts. One twist for the famous in Covey's quadrant diagram is that priority and popularity, although not synonymous, are much more closely related. Remember the toss theory. Your priorities are the seeds of significance while your popularity can be associated with the fruit of fame. If these two are intertwined, then popularity *is* your priority. You will be more likely to self-destruct because you will do anything to become popular. However, at the other extreme, if you don't focus on being popular, no one will see the work that you have done. So, you must understand how your priorities and your popularity affect one another, then find a way to strike a balance between both.

In addition, people seeking fame are more likely to confuse pressure and pleasure with priority and popularity. I see this all the time, and this misinterpretation will keep you on the hamster wheel going nowhere. People think that because they are busy (pressure), they are increasing their fame, when they really are not going anywhere. In another example, people think that they have increased their fame because they went to a certain party or special event, had a blast, and felt famous for a day (pleasure). In actuality, all they did was have a good time. I can't tell you how many bands I have seen go nowhere because their purpose was really rooted in pleasure, not priority.

So, how do you change the preceding scenarios so that you perform activities that keep you on task? The answer is very simple: quantifiable evidence. You must treat priority and popularity like a court case. After each activity, prove that you have increased in priority or popularity. In the first example, you should note how all the busy work that you did brought you closer to fulfilling priority. Determine how that work truly benefited your purpose in life. In the second example, you can network, exchange information with key people, hand out swag, talk to media personnel, and more. Then, the next day when your online presence has increased, or when your name is in the newspaper, you now have tangible evidence of a popularity increase. I have a friend who is always skeptical of my "adventures." When I tell him about something I did, his usual response is, "Pics, or it didn't happen." It's a bit of a joke between us, but that mantra can be serious business for your fame. Time is a lot like money; you should plan your use of it and then evaluate how you spent it. Analyze these four areas of your time, and devise a way to measure your efforts in a manner that proves that each time area is being properly utilized. Don't expect people to assume your fame. Prove it.

PERSONNEL MANAGEMENT

These days, the star life requires many other people besides yourself who are working at your stardom. With that in mind, you will need to be able to select and manage these people well to receive the optimum benefit of the extra help. Doing so, however, is no easy task, and I have had countless plans fall apart due to inadequate help from others. People are all different, with individual thoughts and agendas. They have different beliefs, interests, motivators, aspirations, and more. Successfully getting them all to work together with the same focus, while neglecting themselves to help you achieve is nothing short of amazing. Nevertheless, many of the famous have done well with their core of supporters, and it is not impossible to effectively solicit the help of others. In fact, we have already covered the basic idea of understanding. We just need to apply that idea to others with a macro prospective. In other words, to properly select and manage other people, you will need to understand them in a general communal manner, just as you have spent time here learning about yourself on an individual level.

Timing

People can be very volatile and temperamental, but you can still succeed with them by using the same ideas of timing and motivation. In terms of timing, it is my experience that many people tend to arrive late, especially if there are no consequences. You should set a consequence for tardiness or tell people that an event starts earlier than it actually does to accommodate for their lateness.

Also, don't expect people to be as flexible as you are individually. Flexibility in your schedule and flexibility in a group of schedules are two different things. You will get more help when you time things as conveniently as possible. An inconvenient time will only reduce motivation. Consider how many schedules will be altered by a change in your schedule before making that change. Or better yet, plan your schedule even more carefully so that the likelihood of change is reduced.

Lastly, people can also be "flaky," and you only need to spend a short amount of time in Los Angeles to confirm that. People will agree to something and then back out at the last minute for legitimate reasons or no reason at all. Always be on the lookout for replacements who you can call at a moment's notice. Always have a plan B, C, and D when it comes to people. Don't restrict contact to the virtual space either, no matter how convenient it is. By that, I mean that people can hide behind text messages, emails, and other electronic forms of communication. They will say the right things in the virtual world and be a problem for you in the real world. Meet them in person or at the very least have a phone conversation before working with them. Even the person who seems most committed can leave you at a critical moment.

Motivation

In addition to timing, the people who work with you need to be motivated. They can be motivated by fame, praise, self-fulfillment, and more, but the common and most effective motivator is money. Money is so interesting and important in the life of someone in the spotlight. It greases the wheels of fame and allows you to acquire the manpower and resources for production. Still, money is not the only motivator. Everyone is different, and some may not be motivated by the amount of money you provide, while others may not be motivated by it at all. Either way, attempting to receive without giving something to the person who is helping is the sign of an amateur. Offer a worthwhile motivation, couple it with well-planned timing, and you will receive the help you need.

Maturity

In the management of self and others, there is something to be said about maturity. Maturity is not an automatic result of aging, and I can introduce you to some of the oldest children you have ever seen in Hollywood. Instead, maturity in relation to fame is about smoothing out your journey by applying these concepts, learning from experience, and making wise management decisions. The mature person does not live in ridiculous drama, going from crisis to crisis. They take measures ahead of time to prevent disaster. Their life is not just about having fun, getting their way, or doing whatever feels good. They are not followers. Instead, they lead and set the standard. Mature stars handle themselves personally and don't whimsically hand over the reins of their life to someone else. They understand the complexities of people and plan accordingly. A personnel issue or any other external incident does not ruin their project, because they have multiple contingency plans ready for implementation. Mature stars understand that people are relationships not robots, and they handle each associate with compassion despite hurts of the past. They balance their lives and make time for what's important. Maturity regarding inner personal management and outer personnel management is a sign of growth, and growth will keep you in the spotlight.

■□■□■

As we move to the next section of the book with a focus on public life and more external issues, do not neglect the crucial foundational topics we have covered regarding the five components of identity, their structure, and their management in yourself and others. The public life is very fun and attractive with a different set of rules, but it does not discount your need for a strong established private life. Success in the private realm is what enables your public persona to flourish. A stellar public life in the spotlight is the result of a stellar private life crafted in the dark. Growth in the private life, however, is not pretty. It is full of starts and stops, ups and downs, successes and failures, trials and errors, and wins and losses. It is the place for research and experimentation before you present the final product to the masses.

You will want to draw a line in the sand that works for your particular situation and separates your private and public life so that your best work can be on display. Additionally, people in the new information-age public realm will want to delve into the details of your private life, and you can disrupt the order of your personal world by letting them get too close. After the whirlwind of public life, the private life should be a place of retreat where the foundational message is central and mistakes are allowed. Being able to create and manage these two parallel but separate worlds is a formula for success, and having control on a personal level will protect you from the out-of-control life of fame!

Works Cited

1 (Maslow 370-96)

2 (*NIV*, Matt. 7:16)

3 (Covey 151)

SECTION II:
THE LIGHT

6
THE LIFE OF A STAR

Fame put simply is the condition of being well-known or recognized by many people.[1] By this very definition, it is a selfish endeavor. Fame is all about you. In fact, the desire to be famous as a source of personal empowerment usually comes as a reaction to an unfavorable or adverse past. In a BBC news article, University of Manchester Institute of Science and Technology Professor Cary Cooper explains the findings of his research of fame, stating, "Famous people have usually experienced a negative event during childhood – often it's the loss of a parent, or rejection from a key figure in their life at a younger age."[2] The article goes on to cite Canadian psychologist Mark Schaller's argument that "exposure to fame inevitably produces psychological disturbance."[2] Now, I am sure this is a bit heavier than what you were expecting. How did we go from being a star to psychological disturbance? Well, that is the same question celebrities ask themselves as they meander in and out of the revolving door that is rehab. These kinds of issues arise all too often when we esteem fame so highly, yet the benefits of the life change that comes along with fame can be illusionary.

THE PROPERTIES OF FAME

Fame Appears To Be A Problem-Solver

You may think, "When I become famous, all of my money troubles will be over." Or perhaps your thought is, "People will truly love me when I become famous." The reality, however, is that these issues are too deep for a simple fame fix. If you feel like no one loves you; if you feel like you don't have enough money; if you feel worthless or unaccomplished, these feelings will not go away once you become famous. In fact, fame raises your self-consciousness to a level that heightens the insecurities that you started with! **Fame does not mend; it only magnifies**. When you look into the crowd, you will see the illusion, but when you look down at yourself, you will see even more clearly that you have the same problems you started with. The only difference is that now everyone can see them. **The blinding light of fame is also expository**.

Fame Is Illusory

Fame also carries the illusion of success. When you are famous, people often say that you have "made it." You are worthy of acclaim, and your life is meaningful. But is that really the case? Well, that's what I originally thought until I started chasing fame myself, and I learned that fame is a bottomless pit. Fame is like chasing the horizon; it has no beginning and no end. You are only always in the process of being famous. It is not a plateau that you reach, and instead it is more like a sliding scale with degrees that is difficult to measure due to numerous variables.

Fame Is Subject To Personal Opinion

One may consider you famous while another may not know who you are, and that attribute of fame really hit home with me the day I played piano at Union Station in Los Angeles. I was with a new friend who had never heard me play, and I thought I would just show him what I could do. Now, I considered my fame to be minimal at best, but I was at least somewhat accomplished. Prior to this impromptu performance, I had toured the country, appeared in music videos and a reality TV show, and performed for crowds of up to 18,000. As I played at Union Station, a large crowd gathered, and people began to pull out their phones to take photos and videos of me. However, after I finished playing, a woman came up to me and said, "So, are you ever going to do anything with your talent?" Now, I know she wasn't trying to be mean, but the range of emotions that flowed through me were multitudinous. I was angry, confused, irritated, hurt, and discouraged all at the same time. I didn't know how to react. After all the hard work, after all the performances, after all the photo shoots, after all the interviews, after all the autograph sessions, I was still a nobody in her eyes. To her, I still wasn't famous. I thought that I had reached a certain plateau, but when it comes to fame "…when we get there, there disappears."[3] Fame is wonderful, but do not base your success or your life's worth on it. It is too elusive, too flimsy, and too dependent on the subjectivity of others.

Fame Is Environmentally Relative

Fame is relative to your environment, so amongst a larger pool of participants, your fame diminishes. For instance, a catfish in a fishbowl is so large that it overwhelms its environment. On the other hand, a catfish in a pond is comparatively small. The environment overwhelms it. In a more personal example, I received my primary and secondary schooling in Montgomery, AL. I never considered myself to be the cool or popular kid in school, but my musical abilities did make me famous. If you mentioned my name back home, people knew who I was. However, after moving out to Los Angeles for college, and afterwards developing my career there, the pool of people who were considered to be famous obviously widened significantly. My fame relative to my new environment was virtually insignificant, and I became a small fish comparatively as the competition and opposition to my fame increased. Environment is a factor that heavily influences your fame. **Make it a point to conquer progressively larger fishbowls before you take on the ocean**.

Fame Is Drug-Like

The grandiose nature of fame is like a drug that blurs the lines of reality and makes you feel incredible. However, the desire for fame is insatiable. It draws upon greed within you. As soon as you achieve it at some level, you want more of it. You are never famous enough, and you become jealous of the success of others. We can all fall into this trap so easily, and I even find myself often belittling my past accomplishments. I have thrown some of my works in the trash, and at the time of this writing, my awards sit in boxes collecting dust. Why? Because fame says that what you did yesterday is old news, unworthy of recognition. Fame is all about the here and now. Your job is never done. Through all the glitz and glamour, fame is work, hard work. It requires your constant attention, and within fame you can lose the details of life. It is a road to neglect that sends so many celebrities spiraling out of control right before our eyes. Fame is unstable, and you cannot have a stable life based on instability.

Fame Is Brief

The height of fame is usually brief, and the people who have careers in fame for 10 or 20 years are the exception to the rule. The average musician, actor, sports figure, dancer, or other aspirant has a small window of peak time in the spotlight. They only get a few years if they are lucky, with the height of their success lasting for only one of those years. This occurs because fame is constantly progressing to the next new thing. Fame used to be a bit more permanent, but with the evolution of our society into industrialized, cookie-cutter systems, the assembly line of stardom has continually increased in speed. In *The Fame Formula*, author Mark Borkowski describes the evolution of the fame experience in this manner:

From the cottage industry of the early days to the slick operation of the studio system to Rogers & Cowan's multinational, multitasking outlook, the fame game has always run like a production line. The products, be they canned soup or pop stars, art or actors, are carefully processed. The only difference being that the actors and pop stars can be processed at a place of their choosing. The fame industry is a factory, and like all good businessmen, the managers keep a careful eye on the future. When asked who his favorite client was, Warren Cowan simply said, "The next one!"[4]

Fame Can Be Objectifying And Impersonal

There may be times where you will be treated more like a product than a person, with a demand for you to produce. To handle this kind of treatment, you should view fame as a working environment, not a dwelling place. Charles Cross, for instance, described Jimi Hendrix's trip to Africa as a "reprieve from fame."[5] Now, why would someone need a vacation from something so seemingly wonderful? To many of us, fame appears to be a constant vacation in itself, but along with the outer glamour comes a constant inner pull on your faculties and abilities that can absolutely drain you. Even Marilyn Monroe, one of Hollywood's most iconic figures had some interesting words regarding fame: "Fame will go by and, so long, I've had you, fame. If it goes by, I've always known it was fickle. So at least it's something I experience, but that's not where I live."[6] In fact, if you read other quotes from Marilyn Monroe, it would seem that she felt trapped by the life she lived, yearning for true love, real relationships, respect, and a higher sense of dignity and humanity. So, think of fame as fun work, not real life. In the light, you focus on your persona, but in the dark you should make time for your person.

Although this introduction to fame may appear to be negative, just view it as just the warning label on the package of the toy you are about to play with. I'm not trying to discourage you from being famous, but as we saw in the toss theory, **fame should be the fruit of your tree, not a substitute for your foundation**. Again, these truths echo in the words of Marilyn Monroe: "My work is the only ground I've ever had to stand on. I seem to have a whole superstructure with no foundation, but I'm working on the foundation."[7] This is just a reality check, an attempt to dispel the myths and misconceptions before you launch head first into the unknown. If fame was completely negative, we wouldn't continue to crave it. Fame is actually exciting, but it is also like fireworks: it can be a wonderful, exhilarating experience, or you can get your hand blown off! The picture of your fame, however, will be colored by your motives and expectations.

THE PURPOSE OF FAME

As we discussed earlier, the desire for fame typically doesn't spring out of thin air. There is usually a powerful motivating factor which drives that desire and likely stems from one or several of what I call the four *E's*: eminence, esteem, escape, or extras. Take a look at the descriptions of each of the four *E's* below, and determine which one(s) you can relate to.

The Four *E's*

1. Eminence
If you seek fame for eminence, then you are trying to elevate yourself. Your desire for fame stems from the desire to change your place in the hierarchy of life. You want to be an important person and obtain a social prominence and superiority above others.

2. Esteem
Esteem is perhaps the most common reason people desire fame. If this is your reason, then you want to be acknowledged, accepted, and loved. You desire fame because it will make you feel better about yourself.

3. Escape
You may view fame as an escape from something or someone negative in your "normal" life. You think that if you are famous you won't have to deal with him or her anymore. Or perhaps, when you are on stage, it is like you are a different person whose life is better for at least that moment. **When you don't like your reality, you live in the fantasy of fame**.

4. Extras
If you desire fame for the extras, you are drawn to its real or perceived perks. You see fame as the gateway to more money, preferential treatment, access to more desirable mates, and more.

Just like fame, all four *E's* are selfish. They are attempts to increase yourself. But, is this really so wrong? Is it wrong to want more money or a better place in life? I don't think so. Those are some of the reasons I have wanted to be famous. So, what's the problem? Balance. If these selfish desires are your only goals for fame, it signifies an imbalanced, inward, and possibly misinformed focus. However, if you give these desires a lesser role, with an understanding of what fame can and cannot do for you, you can look beyond yourself and achieve something bigger than fame.

In my studies, I also found that a selfish primary motive for fame can have surprisingly opposite, self-destructive results. I call this the fame box paradox, and you can understand the concept if you think of fame as a box with a length, width, and depth. The three dimensions of this box are described below, and you will see that the bigger you try to make the box, the smaller it becomes.

The Fame Box Paradox

Length

Length represents how long your fame lasts, and a selfish motive for fame limits the lasting effects of your fame. In relation to the toss theory, you would produce the fruit of fame, but there would be no seeds of significance. If there is no seed, once your fruit is eaten, there is no more. In other words, once you end, so does your fame. You have not helped or inspired anyone. Therefore, no one has a reason to continue to spread your fame, and it dies along with you.

Width

Width represents how far-reaching your fame is, or how many people consider you to be famous. A selfish motive for fame here is counterproductive because it erodes any cache you may be building. It starts a chain of negative events that stunts the growth of your fame. Put simply, selfishness causes people to dislike you. When people dislike you, they are less attracted to what you have to offer. When people are less attracted to you, you are less known. And finally, when you are less known, you are less famous.

Depth

Depth represents the substantiality or the impact of your fame in the lives of the people to whom you are famous. Selfish motives for fame give your fame an air of triviality. You may be a thought in people's minds, but you have no place in their hearts. You establish deeper roots when your fame is dedicated to giving back to the people who gave you your fame. And, when you can connect with people on that level, you gain significance in their lives, making your fame and the perpetuation of your fame more important.

So how do you act unselfishly when fame is a selfish endeavor? You seek a nobler priority that makes you famous in the process, and that something else is influence or the fifth E: effect.

The Fifth E: Effect

If you desire fame for effect, you are trying to make a change, leave a mark. You are trying to benefit society in some way. The fifth E is a product of the tree of stable stardom. It is a desire of purpose fulfillment that springs from your roots and propels you not *to* fame, but *through* fame into influence. If you desire effect, then fame isn't actually your primary desire. It is just a necessary door you must go through in order to accomplish your purpose on the biggest possible stage. Those who seek effect are not primarily or obsessively focused on fame. If you are growing into the person that you are to be, fame will be just a byproduct of your efforts. **You don't have to chase fame if you chase growth; when you become a giant, everyone will eventually see you**.

THE PERILS OF FAME

The perils of fame are not as daunting as the title suggests. Instead, they basically are the results of my observations and experiences regarding issues associated with notoriety that have the potential to disrupt your life and/or sabotage your fame. Often, people enter the spotlight with no idea of what to expect. Even I jetted off to Los Angeles with a suitcase, a smile, and visions of sunshine, palm trees, and beautiful women. However, I had no knowledge of the pitfalls and potential traps that lay before me. The effect of your career on your personal life and vice versa can really cause conflict internally and externally if you have not considered the predicaments you might find yourself in due to fame. Below I have outlined 12 of the most common situations I have encountered in hopes that you will think critically regarding your circumstance and create an action plan that will enable you to successfully maneuver through these issues.

Skepticism and Amazement

As you enter the arena of fame your encounters may be quite polarizing. Some people will doubt you, your reasons for being famous, or that you are famous at all! You must be confident in yourself in order to look past these skeptics and continue to do what you feel called to do. On the other hand, you will meet people who are completely amazed at you and what you do. Their admiration will be borderline worship, and you must also be able to humbly deal with these kinds of responses. Find a middle ground. Don't let skeptics pull you down too low, but don't let admirers puff you up too much.

Guilt Trips

Guilt trips occur when people make you feel guilty in order to get you to do something. They are quite common when it comes to just about any level of success, so it is a difficulty that you will probably have to address early on. However, what makes guilt trips even harder to handle is that they usually come from someone close to you. Guilt trips are a prime tool for someone who has enough of an emotional investment in you to make you feel guilty enough to act. This could be a parent, sibling, close friend, or significant other. Still, if anyone wants to make you feel guilty for their own gain, they are manipulating you. Don't allow anyone to do this to you. You are a person, not a puppet. It's wrong, and you will pay a price down the line for allowing it to happen.

Crazymakers

Crazymakers is a term coined by Julia Cameron in her book *The Artist's Way*. As the name suggests, crazymakers are people who make your life crazy, unnecessarily surrounding you in the turmoil they create. Cameron explains the crazymaker symptoms:

> Crazymakers break deals and destroy schedules, expect special treatment, discount your reality, spend your time and money, triangulate those they deal with (setting people against one another in order to maintain their own power position dead center), are expert blamers, create drama — but seldom where it belongs, and hate schedules except their own.[8]

Again, these people can be close to you, but you have to put your foot down, or things will get out of hand. **The drama belongs in your art, not in your life**.

Redundancy

An understanding of fame requires an understanding of people, because they are the ones who give you fame. And, one important general characteristic of people is that they are creatures of habit. When people find something that they like, they want it again and again, the exact same way it was the first time. Now, even though you are a person who grows and changes, your audience will still expect the same things they remember from you. They will attempt to trap you in a time capsule just as they remembered you the last time they saw you, so gauge your audience in regards to this. If you are a comedian, they will want to hear that one joke that always makes them laugh. If you are a musician, a riot will start at your concert if you don't play the hit song. And, it better be just like the record. This is not to say that you can never do something new. Some people, like the singer Pink for example, have made radical changes and still kept an audience. However, your chances for success increase if you evolve gradually so that people can grow to like you more in stages. At times, you might be stuck doing the same thing over and over again, but if that's what the people like, consider it part of the price you pay for fame. Even so, if they like you that much, then you have obviously made a deep connection. Never resent that.

Attachments

An attachment is anyone or anything that partners with you in some way. It could be a company with a product, an organization with a cause, a person who wants to be in your entourage, or even a fellow celebrity who wants to start dating you. Attachments are very common as your name grows. Cross again describes Jimi Hendrix's frustrations with these types of issues: "…there existed numerous groups who sought to attach themselves to him for reasons of race; some suggested he owed something to the black community…"[9] Treat all attachments with a two-way-street mentality. Anything or anyone that is attached to you is receiving something from you, whether you realize it or not. Likewise, you should be receiving something from them as well. If you don't, they are only dead weight. Any attachment that does not contribute, always taking and never giving, is a leech. Recognize leeches and get rid of them quickly.

Drugs

The life of fame puts an unbelievable stress on your mind and body. It is a life of intense pressure and overwhelming anxiety. So, how does one cope with all of this? Enter: the drug dealer. Fame gives you access to many things, and drugs are near the top of that list. It's simple supply and demand. There are drugs to help you go to sleep, drugs to keep you awake, drugs to make you feel good, and drugs to make you stronger. This list goes on and on. Stars crave remedies to these types of issues, and drugs are viable solutions for them. The problem, however, is that people in the spotlight, generally speaking, are more prone to addiction. According to Dr. Scott Teitelbaum, an associate professor and vice chair of the University of Florida psychiatry department, celebrity drug addiction is linked to a developed narcissism, which includes objection to regulation and rules.[10] Celebrities then validate their drug usage because they feel different, special, or above the law.[10] Additionally, the medical director for psychiatric services at Lake Charles

Memorial Hospital, Dr. Dale Archer has observed that after famous people come down off the high of doing whatever makes them famous, drug usage is the common method implemented to keep that high going so that they don't feel the letdown.[10] So if you think you have a drug problem, get help now! The list of celebrities whose careers and/or lives have been cut short because of drug issues is painfully long. Learn from their mistakes. Incorporate the toss theory and seek natural remedies before turning to drugs.

Sex

Fame can make you more sexually desirable, while positioning you to encounter a greater number of sexually desirable partners. It sounds pretty good...until something goes wrong. As we have seen for example with President Bill Clinton and Monica Lewinsky, people can know you more by who you may or may not have had "sexual relations" with than the great things you have done. When you are famous, you should definitely view sex as any other attachment, carefully choosing a sexual partner. Sex requires opening up, a letting down of the guard. Yes, it can be a beautiful expression of love, or it can be a prime avenue of attack. When you are in the spotlight, you will have to consider the motives of your sexual partners. Do they love you? Are they using you to enhance their own stardom? Do they want to blackmail you? Do they want your money? It can feel right at the time, but if things go wrong, it can totally jeopardize your career and reputation. You can contract sexually transmitted diseases, find yourself in embarrassing sex tapes, produce illegitimate children, end up fighting rape allegations, or lose your mojo and endorsements. Sex when famous breaks down the barrier of your private life and allows your public life to cross over. This is very shaky ground, and you should always be cautious with your sexual partners.

Gossip

If you cannot handle people talking about you now, then you will struggle greatly with it in the spotlight. Gossip is a huge part of fame, and there are entire industries dedicated to celebrity gossip. As your popularity grows, you will inevitably become a topic of people's conversation. However, what is said may be painfully true, not completely accurate, or just totally false. If you can, try not to read or listen to unfounded gossip about yourself. This will only make you feel self-conscious and reinforce untruths within yourself. However, gossip means that you are on people's minds, and that is a good thing.

Ill Intentions

If you think everyone is going to enjoy and accept your fame as much as you will, then you are truly mistaken. Your fame may make you the talk of the town, but in the process, it will also make you a target. People will see your fame as an opportunity to bring up your negative past, harm you or your family physically, steal from you, blackmail you, sue you, and more. Reality TV stars Heidi Montag and Spencer Pratt agree that some people will even just want to be you or take your place:

> There's always someone beneath you who wants your job. If you're the starting quarterback for the Cowboys, the backup wants your job. If you're the manager of McDonald's, the assistant manager wants your job. And if you're a celebrity, there are people out there who want to take your spotlight.[11]

Don't live in paranoia, but at the same time, don't be naïve. Jealous people will want to bring you down with or without good reason. Even if you are the nicest person in the world, you can still become the object of someone else's hate.

As a side note, don't constantly mention the people who hate you, or your "haters," as they are commonly referred to these days. This is really overused and tacky, and it makes you look conceited. Even if you have so-called haters, you show a certain unnecessary preoccupation by continuously mentioning them. When you talk about these haters, you give them power. Keep doing your own thing, keep yourself protected, and don't give them the time of day.

These stars have been attacked on stage.[12]	These stars have had their homes burglarized.[13]
Britney Spears	Paris Hilton
Rihanna	Audrina Patridge
Justin Bieber	Rachel Bilson
Demi Lovato	Orlando Bloom
Robbie Williams	Lindsay Lohan
Avril Lavigne	Megan Fox
These stars have had their personal information hacked.[14]	These stars have been sued multiple times.[15]
Jude Law	Oprah Winfrey
Vanessa Hudgens	David Letterman
Scarlett Johansson	Sacha Baron Cohen
Mila Kunis	Perez Hilton
Miley Cyrus	Tom Cruise
Jessica Alba	Beyoncé
Sofia Vergara	Jennifer Lopez

Figure 6-1

Unrealistic Expectations

For some reason, when you are famous, people will often project a superhero-like persona onto you. For instance, they may expect you to know everything about everything, but if there is something you don't know about, try to avoid it. If you give foolish answers, you run the risk of developing iconic embarrassing moments like the Miss South Carolina Teen USA contestant who froze up and gave a bumbling, incoherent answer during the 2007 pageant.[16] If you are unable to do something, just make a priority choice and explain your reasons. Anyone who discounts your personal justifications is treating you like a product, not a person. Always shoot for peak performance, but understand yourself enough to know what you can and cannot do.

Misinterpretations

No matter how clear you think your message is, it still has to travel through someone else's eyes and ears, meaning that everything you say and do is subject to interpretation. Just assume that most people are not on the same wavelength as you and make your statements as simple and clear as possible. If you go for the lowest common denominator, you will be able to extend your reach to the broadest range of people. In regards to this peril, it wouldn't hurt to take some notes from the marketing profession. They are masters at analyzing a product and creating a clear, consistent message that entices you to buy. **Don't just do; test everything**. The reaction of others is just as important as your own opinion.

Demand

Despite the private and personal lines you have drawn, people will always try to cross them. If you are in high demand, I encourage you to learn a great little two-letter word: No! If you are asked to do something that does not line up with your purpose and goals, does not fit into your schedule, or jeopardizes you or others in some other way, then don't be afraid to say "no." This differs from unrealistic expectations in that it may refer to something you probably should not do even though you may be able. **Increased demand requires increased stability**. The less you are in control of your life, the more demand will eat you alive. You must understand your own limits and your own tree of stable stardom to determine if you can live up to the demands that are being placed on you.

THE PROTECTORS OF FAME

Now that we have covered many of the properties, purposes, and perils of fame, you can see how fame is a very valuable, yet extremely volatile asset. Fame isn't something that can be left to develop on its own. Fame means that you are getting attention, and getting attention requires your attention. That bucket of fame is always leaking, and there's no way to stop it. Naturally, your fame is always diminishing. However, even though you can't stop it, you can slow it down. If you want your fame bucket to last a long time, you need to constantly pour into it and patch holes wherever you can. In other words, yes, fame is weak, but there are measures you can take to protect it.

Insulation

Insulation is a great way to protect yourself and your fame. It means putting up a shield, a barrier to safeguard whatever is important to you. Whether it be for your personal life, your property, your money, or your family, insulation will give you peace of mind during the fame experience regarding the things you hold dear. For example, your insulation can be a bodyguard to protect you from the public, an agent that keeps you out of heated negotiation, or a private bank account to handle your confidential transactions. It can be a secluded house to limit fan and media access, or a list of questions you will not discuss in interviews. Additionally, written contracts are also great forms of insulation…pun intended.

Creativity

Your own creativity is an excellent fame protector because it causes you to stand out. And, when you continue to stand out, you ensure fame at some level. Don't get too caught up in trying to be like everyone else. The people who stand out the most are the people who are different. Creativity draws on your individuality, what is uniquely you. And once you internalize that, you can creatively utilize it for the protection of your fame.

Education

They key to using education to protect your fame is working with the mentality that instead of just being educated, you are always educating. In the same regard, don't limit yourself to formal schooling; that is only one form of education. Quite often, school can be a validating place of learning for those who are unmotivated in doing. And, with the right motivation, I have learned more outside of school than in it. There are many other ways to learn. You can travel the world and experience new cultures, or you can go to seminars or read books. You can subscribe to trade magazines, speak with mentors, or watch television programs that focus on your particular field, but don't limit yourself to just your area of expertise. Consider the breadth of your education as well. A broad knowledge of subjects will allow you to connect with many people on many levels. Education is paramount, especially in this information age where you may quickly be left behind.

Elevation (Upward Growth)
Elevation or upward growth simply refers to becoming better at what you do. A principle of this natural world is that everything in it decays and declines, so you should constantly find quantifiable ways to improve yourself in order to stay ahead. If you seem stuck in the same place all the time, never increasing your fame, it may be a sign that you are underdeveloped. Additionally, as other people grow around you, your lack of growth will become even more apparent. Continue a cycle of practicing and doing. An advanced talent is usually more attractive and more conducive to fame.

Expansion (Outward Growth)
Expansion is outward growth in other areas related to your main focus, and this creates many avenues for your fame to increase. Singers and rappers are incredible examples of this in that after solidifying a music career, many branch out into merchandising, movies and television, toys, video games, restaurants, real estate, writing, public speaking, and more. Someone may not like your music, but they might be fond of your acting ability. Others may just happen to pick up a copy of your autobiography at the bookstore and get to know you that way, having never seen your modeling. Expansion constantly creates ways for people to stumble upon you; however, **you should never expand outward until you have had significant upward growth**. Outward growth is an overflow, and there is no overflow from an empty cup. If you only have limited ability and resources, then you should concentrate it in one area. But, when you have increased ability and resources, there will be more to spread around elsewhere. When you feel like you have reached capacity, that is when you should expand.

Delegation
Another way to protect your fame is understanding that you cannot do everything by yourself. You need help to be and remain famous while still maintaining some sanity. Even Jesus had disciples! Still, don't get caught up in delegation just for the prestige or just for the convenience. Paying someone to pick out the green M&M's is not what delegation is all about. However, an agent who obtains work for you or a publicist who puts you in

the news are great places to begin when you are ready. If your delegation does not increase your ability, or bottom line, it is unnecessary. Also, if you start off immediately with delegation, you run the risk of someone taking advantage of you. Before acquiring help, you should do and learn as much as you can on your own. Then, when you need something done, you will know all about how it should be done. Delegation is an example of the personnel management we discussed in the previous chapter. Make sure you have a handle on timing and motivation before selecting help.

Counsel

I can't emphasize enough that being famous today is not a one-man job. In addition to advising a team of people below through delegation, you will need a team of advisors above to help you make the best decisions. It can be difficult to see in the bright light of fame, but several different viewpoints will give you a clearer overall picture of yourself and your surroundings. A good group of counselors will give you life through genuine relationship. They will be a supportive and encouraging haven in which you can share your inner-most thoughts and feelings. A group of advisors is standard in any large undertaking, and you should view your fame in the same manner. The president has a presidential cabinet, CEO's have a board of directors, and spiritual leaders have mentors or "fathers" in the faith. Once you determine your strengths and weaknesses, you will be able to decide on what help you need.

Vigilance

It can be so easy to live in your own little world when fame requires so much focus on yourself. However, you should make it a point to know as much as possible about what is going on around you in order to protect your fame. Consider what is happening globally, nationally, and locally, inside and outside of your field. How will current events affect you? What pitfalls can you avoid? How can you take advantage of certain opportunities? Seek to ally yourself with associates or worthy causes. Look for available positions that will elevate your career. And, be aware of trends on which you may capitalize. Don't just be satisfied with the status quo. Keep your eyes and ears open, and direction will present itself in your journey

Mystery

Nothing captures attention like a good mystery, and mysterious elements about your fame will intrigue your audience and prevent them from becoming bored with you. Don't feel obligated to tell everyone everything; reserve a few secrets and keep people guessing. For example, being a quiet person has coincidentally drummed up a world of mystery around me. I am just a naturally quiet individual, but it is almost comical to see people ruminate on what I may be thinking or feeling. There are so many ways to add mystery, and your unique individuality is a natural starting point. Your sexuality, your dress, your work, your friends, and just about anything else you can think of can be turned into a curiosity that draws attention. Your mystery is a magnet that will bring people to you, so don't be afraid to play off the intrigue of others.

Visibility

Visibility may seem like a no-brainer, but its relationship to fame is too often misunderstood. First, it's important to understand that visibility and fame are not synonymous. Visibility is the precursor to fame. And once you are famous, visibility continues to act as a protector by keeping your image fresh in the minds of the public. If fame is the condition of being well-known, then visibility can be described as the condition of being well-seen.

Fame requires a connection to the audience that enables them to identify and remember you over and over again. If you make a network television appearance, you are not automatically famous. You are visible; you are seen. It is the impact of that appearance that creates fame. Without impact that establishes you as a recognizable figure, you are only seen and not known, visible, not famous. However, even with impact, a one-time appearance is not enough. People will need to see you again and again before they remember you or are able to be moved to action. I believe there is no such thing as too much visibility, and with today's technological advances, you or your works can be seen in multiple places simultaneously, circumventing the exhausting efforts that may be required to be physically present.

At the peak of their career, musical group The Black Eyed Peas were seemingly everywhere. I saw them in music videos, magazines, and commercials; I watched them at community events, award shows, and festivals; I heard them on radios, store sound systems, and car stereos. It was no secret that visibility was a high priority for them, and their long career and recognizable status proves that it served them well. Keep in mind, however, that you don't have to be at the level of The Black Eyed Peas to build visibility. It is something you can definitely plan on your own. But, when you get to a level of delegation, a good marketing person should be able to maintain and enhance your presence in the public.

Accessibility

Before you go overboard with insulation and mystery, make sure that you are still in some ways accessible to your fans. Being accessible can be more impactful than you realize, and a single personal moment can make a deep connection. U.S. presidents shake hands and kiss babies on the campaign trail because it shows a connection to the people. It effectively humanizes them as they take on such an extraordinarily elite position. Most people understand that you are busy, so when you make time for them, it speaks volumes. Sign autographs, take photos, shake hands, and give hugs until you are worn out. If you turn your back on people, they will quickly do the same, so **try not to put yourself above the people in this area whenever possible**. Accessibility gives you the opportunity to provide a personal touch, to create a significant moment in the life of another, and that means you have influenced. This not only protects your fame; it also exponentially increases it.

Neology

Neology is the use of a new word or expression or of an established word in a new or different sense.[17] Creating a new word or being associated with its propagation can be an amazing and often overlooked boost for your fame. The interesting component of this protection of fame is the automatic historical element that it creates. For example, although the word *bootylicious* was originally coined by the rapper Snoop Dogg, the term recently made its way into the Oxford English Dictionary, further cementing the fame of R&B group Destiny's Child who popularized the term in their 2001 hit song. Over 5,000 words are added to the English language yearly.[18] Your name, your actions, your products, and more can be morphed into new words that meander into the common vernacular.

■□■□■□

The private life and the public life differ greatly, so finding a point at which both can exist and flourish is an extremely difficult balancing act. Your personal life thrives in stability and control, while fame is a friend of instability and chaos. Yes, fame is one giant, long-lasting party, but its extremes can be downright scary. Your personal life is directed by you, but fame is directed by others. It might be a good idea to re-evaluate your reasons for pursuing fame now that you understand what it entails.

There seems to be no one method to obtaining fame as it lends itself less and less to formula. There is no rhyme or reason to its madness and who it is bestowed upon. Yes, after decades of strenuous work you may become famous, or you could become famous instantly through association or relation, walking right into glitz and glamour with little or no work at all. And even if fame is granted, you can be known by millions in one environment while simultaneously being unheard of in another! Fame just isn't fair.

There is formula to opportunity but no set structure to fame, and chasing it is truly a chasing of the wind. Still, don't be discouraged in your journey and continue in your purpose while maintaining a realistic perspective. Fame at its highest level is extremely rare; its definition necessitates anomaly. So, it is important to view fame as a number of stages, not as an on-off switch. It should be measured in degrees, not duality. Fame is your stage, but it is not your entire life. You can have a large stage, or you can have a small stage. Either way, **it may be the quality of your performance, not the size of your platform that eventually matters most**.

Works Cited

1 ("Fame")

2 ("Why Would")

3 (Cameron 182)

4 (Borkowski 258)

5 (Cross 264)

6 ("Marilyn Monroe" 38)

7 (Monroe and Taylor 40)

8 (Cameron 44)

9 (Cross 273)

10 (McGuiness)

11 (Montag and Pratt 77)

12 ("When Fans Attack")

13 (Ghebremedhin)

14 (Lopez)

15 ("Sued Celebs")

16 (Celezic)

17 ("Neology")

18 (Global Language Monitor)

YAY! EVERYBODY LIKES YOU!

These days you often hear the term *it factor* thrown around the circles of fame in an attempt to describe someone who has something special about them that cannot be denied. Since the it factor is so hard to describe, hence the terminology, its meaning has a variety of interpretations. Below, I will outline my own philosophy on the it factor and its components. I have found it to be quite enigmatic, complexly wrapped up in a natural simplicity. However, I hope my perspective will provide clarity and some sense of quantification in a way that will enable you to benefit from its use in your own endeavors.

For me, the *it* in it factor stands for individualistic tantalization. Now, say that five times fast! It sounds a lot more complicated than it is, but there are just two major components. We have already discussed individuality. These are the qualities that set you apart from other people. They are the components that make you unique. Tantalization, or the act of tantalizing refers to seduction or enticement. Tantalization is about leaving someone's mouth watering in hopes that they will want more. So, put together, **individualistic tantalization is the display of unique personal qualities in a remarkably attractive manner**.

Both individuality and tantalization are needed for you to have the it factor. It may be difficult to understand how both components work together, so analogy may be best to differentiate the two:

Your individuality is the attraction, but your tantalization is the advertisement.

Your individuality is the hook, but your tantalization is the worm.

Your individuality is the possession, but your tantalization is the expression.

As you can see, one without the other can lead to either inconspicuousness or disappointment. Attractive individuality without tantalization is like a hidden gem. You might have something great, but there is nothing that steers people toward you. There is no incentive for them to pay attention to you, no reason for them to desire you. In this state, you only make waves with people who just happen to stumble upon you. On the other hand, tantalization without individuality will frustrate your followers. It's like the boy who cries wolf when there is nothing to see. Tantalization alone may get many people to you, but without substance, the ones who stay will be few and far between. In this state, you are all hype, a one-hit wonder, a dish that people will push away after the first bite. However, when you have both qualities working together, your fans will be drawn to you. They will like what they see and will want to come back for more, even if they aren't fully able to explain their captivation. That's what the it factor is all about.

INDIVIDUALITY: THE DISCOVERY

Individuality gives unique detail to your archetype. As human beings, we have so many similar qualities, yet we are all different. Our differences are interesting and can usually help others see differently; however, we are often programmed to hide them. If we stick out, we might be made fun of or shunned by our community. However, our individuality should really give us a sense of purpose, and **you can discover your destiny by developing your differences**. What is uncommon about you? That's where your true value lies. Even your flaws can be advantageous if you use them properly.

Many components of individuality may be genetic, but individuality can also be altered in internal and external ways. For example, I love languages. Now, if I learned how to speak five languages fluently, that would be a significant internal change to my individuality. I would stand out as an individual because most people cannot speak that many languages. I would still look the same; I would still engage in the same popular activities; I would still drive the same car, but I would be different from others around me because of the internal change.

In regards to external changes, a change of residence would be a prime example. We can start with the statement, "I am a black man." Even though that can be considered unique in itself, it is pretty common in most areas of the U.S. to see a black man walking around town. However, if I say, "I am a black man who lives in Iceland," things change. It is uncommon to see a black man in Iceland, and that location change alone skyrockets my individuality even though I have made no internal changes to myself. So, keep in mind that there are several ways to fine-tune your individuality, but internal changes are usually much harder than external ones.

The Gifted Ones

For some people, their individualism just shines automatically. It's like they cannot help being mysterious, funny, intimidating, edgy, etc. Have you ever met someone like that? After spending time with them, you usually say, "wow" afterwards, and you often come away with a strong archetype that encompasses your experience with them. These individualistic attributes, however, aren't always positive, and it's important to establish the difference between a character and real life. For example, some actors have an individual knack for playing villains or jerks, and that is actually an attractive quality for particular acting roles. In real life, however, a mean-spirited jerk does not attract; he repels. Even if a negative individualism draws attention to you, at the end of the day, the heroes are celebrated while the villains are ostracized. Some people are truly gifted with a natural positive individuality, but if you feel like your individuality may be undefined or not confidently expressed, then keep reading!

Undefined Individuality

If your individuality is not defined, your tree of stable stardom has weak roots, specifically in terms of identity. The it factor requires clarity. You need to know what qualities shine the brightest in you, what you believe in, what you like and don't like, what makes you happy, what your natural actions and reactions are, what is important to you, and more. Also, when it comes to these matters, **your individuality can be like the back of your head; you know it's there, but other people will have to tell you what it looks like**. You usually won't have to fish for your individuality. Most of it will just come out naturally, and people will reinforce who you are by telling you.

Unsure Individuality

If you are not confident in your individuality, that means that you are afraid of something. That something usually involves some combination of other people's acceptance of you and your acceptance of yourself. These kinds of confidence issues are typically felt most vividly in your teenage years; however, a life in the spotlight at any age is a lot like high school and its associated pressures. Every day, there is societal stress placed upon you to fit in, to be cool, to be normal, and to basically act like everyone else. For some of us, that pressure alone affects us greatly. But in the spotlight, it is magnified many times over, creating continual conflict with our individuality.

We are all unique, but our basic instinct is to group together. This produces a group mentality which is often counterproductive to the goals of someone who desires to stand in the spotlight. The constant battle of confident individualism is fought against the discounting perspective of society, and there always seems to be a societal denotation for who you are. Individuality says that you are mysterious; society says you are a loner who doesn't fit with the in-crowd. Individuality says you have a strong sexuality; society makes you out to be a slut. Individuality says you are an intellectual; society calls you a nerd. Individuality says you are a superior athlete; society refers to you as a dumb jock. Individuality says you are a jokester; society wonders if you are ever going to grow up. Individuality says that you are devout; society thinks that you're just a stick-in-the-mud! Do you see how there always seems to be something wrong with who you are? That is the battle you fight every day whether you realize it or not, and that is why confidence is so important. I see so many people daily with amazingly unique individual characteristics, but you can tell that they are afraid to let them out for fear of rejection. So many people would change the world if they only had confidence in themselves. It takes a certain audacity to be who you truly are, and it is that same audacity that will make you famous. But even with that confidence, society will wonder why you are so arrogant!

The Real Deal

In your efforts to display your it factor, your individuality should be genuine. Often, we cleverly put up a false individuality to hide our true self. We hope that by doing this, we can guarantee acceptance. I find this to be the case frequently with waiters at restaurants, or really anyone in a customer service position. Some of these people look like if they were any more unnaturally high on life, they would jump up, touch the moon, and start walking on sunshine. However, I can tell that it is a failed attempt at a charade to make me think that they are actually enjoying serving me. I would rather have a real person with a real attitude than someone who paints on a personality like makeup.

Many people put on a show in an attempt to display their it factor. However, if you are not presenting your true character, your audience will sense something fake and be turned off by you. The it factor is so uniquely natural that it really can't be fabricated well. Like they say, you either have *it*, or you don't. Always remember, **the radiation of who you are will outshine who you pretend to be**. Having the individualistic component means being who you truly are at 100%. People who lack this individualistic expression also often use the excuse, "When I become famous, that's when I'll act differently." No. Remember the properties of fame. There is no point where you become famous. You are always being famous to varying degrees. Your fame starts now with your daily interactions. Get to know yourself and have the guts to put the true you out there so that you can understand which societal conformities to accept or reject.

TANTALIZATION: THE DISPLAY

Tantalization is the trappings of your individuality. It is the shiny gift wrapping on your present. Tantalization is that killer outfit. It's the way you walk, the way you talk, and the way you do things. It's not what you are all about, but it entices people to hang around you and see who you are. Tantalization is a radiation. It causes people to approach you, to ask you questions, to flirt with you, or to comment on you. It is a surface layer that gives people a reason to get to know you. Tantalization can be a delicate matter, because any off-putting parts of your tantalization can ruin your whole it factor. **While your individualism is the energy that seeks to push your inner qualities outward to people, tantalization is the energy that seeks to pull people inward to you**. Next, we'll look at five key areas in which tantalization occurs.

Poise

Your poise is your composure, your ability to remain steady and balanced in various situations. It can also often be described as the way you carry yourself. For example, poise can be found in the way you walk. Some walk very quickly, indicating urgency and importance. Others have a slow strut, emanating coolness and casualness. Some women seem to be on the catwalk as they walk down the street, swinging their hips from side to side. They overflow with femininity and a palpable sexual energy. The way you sit is also indicative of your poise. Do you immediately slouch in your chair and put your feet up, or do you sit up straight with your knees locked together? When listening to someone, do you turn towards them, leaning in to catch their every word? Or, do you sit to the side, cross your arms, and occasionally look at the speaker? Poise can also refer to how you handle tense situations. Do you freak out during an emergency or do you address crisis situations as calmly as possible? Will a probing interviewer get under your skin and cause you to react on camera, or will you take the hits and give controlled responses? A lack of poise in any situation can happen to anyone; however, such situations are most common with amateurs and a wrongful outburst can signify the beginning of the end. Therefore, continue to evaluate and develop poise so that you always look like a polished professional.

Poise is about being in control, or at least looking like you are in control over yourself and your environment. Some people, however, pride themselves on not having poise. Television talk show host Conan O'Brien for example is admittedly a lanky, awkward fellow who has poise in other areas but lacks it in his physical movements. However, as a comedian, it is a trait that he uses to get laughs as he makes fun of himself. Still, in most circles, poise is a valuable tool of tantalization that can point to a confident controlled identity. For those of you who perform on a stage, poise is an absolute must, and in this arena, it is often referred to as stage presence. It doesn't matter how good the music sounds if you look awkward and uncomfortable on stage. If you seem like you are not in control, your performance just does not translate well. There are many great singers and musicians who will only go so far because they lack the stage presence, the poise, the tantalization.

Appeal

Appeal is your attraction ability. It refers to certain qualities you possess or actions you perform that stand out from your other attributes and are particularly likeable. Appeal can manifest in several different ways and is also an integral part of defining your target demographic. Your main reason for being famous (singing, acting, dancing, leading, instructing, etc.) will obviously be your main appeal, but other qualities and actions can more clearly define your main audience or enable you to discover a totally new associated audience.

David Beckham's main appeal, for instance, comes from him being one of the world's best soccer players. In his stint with Manchester United, his popularity boosted as he led the team to win an FA Cup and Premiere Division title in the same year. He then won the La Liga championship during his time with Spain's Real Madrid team, simultaneously sending their merchandise sales into the hundreds of millions. And finally, his signing with the L.A. Galaxy led to increased popularization of soccer in America and record-breaking season ticket sales and merchandise sales for the Galaxy. So, the fame-producing ability of his soccer play is duly noted. However, one day I watched Beckham on a daytime talk show with an audience comprised mostly of women who may or may not have been interested in soccer, and his appeal went in a different direction. He mentioned how he cooks and takes his kids to school in the morning, and with each camera close-up of the audience, you could see women just melting in their seats. The audience was swooning and enraptured by the "soft" side of David Beckham. At that moment, there was less of a soccer appeal and more of an emotional appeal.

Beckham grabbed the attention of a completely different audience outside of the typical soccer fan. This alternate appeal, however, was no accident. It purposely played on the desires of the audience. In business terms, it was simply another case of supply and demand. Beckham fulfilled the role and supplied the tough athlete who also had a softer, thoughtful, and compassionate side. On the other hand, the talk show audience had an attraction to and thus a demand for those particular attributes in a man.

It is important to discover not only your main appeal, but also the associate appeals that attract those on the outskirts in order to widen your audience. As a female singer, your primary appeal to women may be the intimacy of your lyrics and the emotion in your singing; however, your primary appeal to men may be your beauty. As a cereal manufacturer, your appeal to children may be bright colors, cartoon characters, and prizes inside the cereal box, but your appeal to parents may be affordability and nutritional value. Your awareness of your identity and the external responses and reactions to you will reveal your strongest appeals. Once you determine those appeals, you can create avenues of tantalization in which you can direct people to them.

MASS APPEAL
VS
★ **TARGETED APPEAL** ★

A TARGETED APPEAL CAN BE SUBSTANTIALLY GREATER THAN A MASS APPEAL.

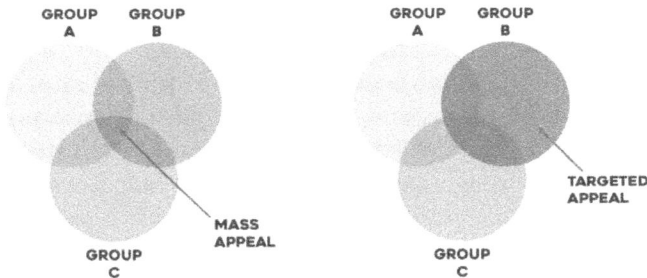

Figure 7-1

Lastly, be aware of the limits of your appeal. Our tastes are becoming more selective as we continue to diversify as a people. With that in mind, you should not exhaust yourself by trying to appeal to every group. **You cannot be everything to everyone**! If you try to do this, you will burn yourself out and lose your identity in the process. The concept of mass appeal refers to appealing to large general groups, not necessarily appealing to everyone. So, depending on your offering, you can actually reach more people with a targeted appeal than with a mass appeal. This occurs because each group that you appeal to always alienates another group to some degree. Your basketball skills as a pure shooter alienate those who like high-flying dunkers. Your flaming-hot salsa recipe alienates those who don't like spicy food. Even this book alienates those who have no desire to be famous. Also, note that widespread fame requires you to appeal to an enormous group or a great number of smaller groups. So, the size of your appeal will greatly influence the degree of your fame.

Approachability

Approachability and appeal work hand in hand in the pursuit of fame; however, it is important to distinguish between and implement both to be successful. Approachability answers the question of how people get to you, and someone who is approachable is easy to access, meet, or talk to. When I'm on television and movie sets, the casts and crews always talk about the stars who are approachable. The fame of approachable stars spreads like wildfire because they instantly extend themselves for deeper connection. Appeal, on the other hand answers the question of why people come to you, and someone who is appealing is attractive, interesting, fascinating, enticing, etc. Appeal is very diverse and subjective, and it usually stems from your natural qualities. We have also already discussed some external methods by which you may add appeal; however, if you think you have no natural appeal, you don't know yourself. There are usually multiple qualities varying in strength that draw people to you, and those draws need to be emphasized in the spotlight. Once you understand them, you will also be able to understand the types of people who will find you appealing. Then, you can create a way for them to get to you. **When you identify your pull of appeal, you can find your pool of audience, and create your path of approachability**.

For example, the popular British comedian Russell Brand has been spotted having breakfast with homeless people and giving away items to others on the street. Performing such acts of kindness shows an incredible level of approachability for a celebrity of his stature. Now, who knows? Maybe Brand's interactions with the homeless may be just a media stunt, but hearing that news story makes you think, "Hey, Russell Brand is a man of the people. Maybe he'll take me out to lunch one day!" Although his quirky individuality is definitely polarizing, the approachability he conveys makes one unafraid of his uniqueness.

In a personal example, I have a confident, leadership aura about me. It's not an alpha male demeanor like the captain of a sports team. Instead, it's just as if I know what I'm doing and where I'm going all the time, even when sometimes I actually don't. It permeates through my mannerisms and causes people to always come to me for help or guidance. When I walk down the street, people *always* ask me for directions. They will pass a crowd and come directly to me! Usually, I know the city well enough to help them, but how do they instinctively know to come to me? The same thing happens to me in grocery stores. I am never wearing a uniform or name tag, and you would think that it would be obvious that I don't work there. Still, people just gravitate to me and begin asking questions. Approachability is very powerful, and **your ability to influence increases greatly when the personal connection comes to you**.

Communication

We already touched on communication in Chapter 4, but here I think it is important to further elaborate on the style of your communication. As someone in the spotlight, you always want to communicate in a style that your audience can appreciate and understand. You may have the right message for the right audience, but if your style is unattractive, offensive, or confusing, your message immediately loses potency. For instance, I could have titled this book, *Life Skills and Business Skills for the Well-Known*. It's a descriptive title, but it has a boring style. *Being Famous*, however, is a catchier title that also immediately points you to my message. And, my hope is that if you like the style of the title, you will also like the style of the book.

In terms of communication, your style comes across in various ways. The tone of your voice can reflect style. Your tone can be polite, commanding, squeaky, or soothing. Your grammar also reflects your style. Do you use slang or proper English? Do you use lots of technical jargon, or are you like me, mixing a variety of different grammatical styles?

Your communication style also shows up in your conversations with others. For example, I know people who talk very fast and will barely let you get a word in. Others pack a wealth of information in very few words. Even the way you answer the phone (Hello? Hi! Yo. What's up? Who is this? Speak to me, peasant.) indicates a communication style. In each case, you really have to understand the person's style in order to clearly receive their message.

To properly convey your identity, you should also be aware of your nonverbal communication style. The clothes you wear, your attitudes, and your facial expressions are all tantalization factors that either draw people in or push them away. Even the simplicity of a smile can express that you are open for communication.

As someone in the spotlight, your style not only has to be clear, but it has to grab attention at the first impression. It will be hard enough to find people who will try you out the first time, but if you don't nail it on the first go around, there most likely will not be a second. The competition is too fierce, and audiences are too savvy and fickle for you to expect two and three chances. If your style does not captivate immediately, people will move on.

If you want to be a rapper, but you have no urban style, it will be very difficult to generate a large appeal. Similarly, a politician who always uses slang and dresses in baggy clothes will most likely not be elected. Even if you have a message that the people would love, your unattractive style will turn them away before they even hear what you have to say.

Manners

Manners may sound like a childish subject to be included here, but you will be amazed at the number of people who lack them and how much a lack of them can affect your career. Fame is a relationship industry, and your requests can often come more from your reputation than your resumé. There are so many incredible musicians who I won't work with anymore because they are rude, have no filter on their language and actions, or have no sense of appropriateness. As I mentioned before, fame can put you in many different social settings with many different types of people, so offending certain people or groups can be limiting or destructive to your fame. There are a wealth of rules, customs, and traditions, but manners really boil down to one word: respect. Manners stem from your identity and your views on how other people are to be treated. They are not meant for yourself. They are a sign of respect to others, and that's why good manners draw people to you. It shows that you care about them, not just yourself.

Fame feeds into your selfish nature and your selfish desires. This can easily result in an inflated ego which may cause you to only use people for your own needs instead of loving them, which requires respect. Focusing only on yourself and your own agenda fosters disconnection and sets the stage for manners to be thrown by the wayside. Everyone has the need for self-esteem just like you do, and manners are one way to show your acknowledgement and appreciation of other people. Opening doors; treating your help well; being a good host; behaving well at the dinner table; respecting the customs of foreigners; and not ignoring, insulting, or intruding upon others all contribute to creating a cycle of relationship development. As you seek to elevate others, they will seek to elevate you and increase your fame.

One day, I was supposed to have a business meeting to pitch one of my musical ideas. After I arrived at the facility, I told the secretary why I was there. She paged the gentleman I was to meet several times, but he didn't show up. The staff was becoming embarrassed about his lateness, but I waited patiently, and about 30 minutes later, he finally appeared. Now, I had many other things to do that day and several other people to meet with as well. I could have put myself first and stormed out in frustration. I could have talked down to the secretary and scolded her for not being able to find the man. I could have even directly held the man's lateness against him during our meeting. But instead, I kept my poise and showed manners. I didn't bring up the matter of the man's lateness. I graciously thanked the secretary for helping me, and I was courteous to the man during the meeting, letting him do all the talking that he needed to do instead of pushing my agenda on him. But, after all of that, he couldn't really help me with my project. It was all a waste of time, right? Wrong. The man said, "Even though I can't take on your music project, I'm still going to help you because I like you." He then proceeded to give me the names and numbers of several of his wealthiest friends. He also took several of my advertisements so that he could mail them to other people he knew. And, as I walked out the door, I overheard him commenting to his co-workers about what a nice young man I was. He did all of that without even hearing a single note of my music. He was so impressed with the quality of my person that he immediately trusted the quality of my product.

Small gestures in manners and etiquette did a lot to increase my fame that day, and they can do the same for you. Use manners to overcome the celebrity stereotype of vanity and self-centeredness. Remember, people will use these little interactions with you, these small portions of life, to make generalizations about you entirely. **Your ability to shine light on the world shows that you are not a distant star; instead it conveys that you are striving to achieve the closeness and warmth of the sun!**

■□■□■□■

The it factor has typically been thought of as a very natural gift, but it can be and often is developed over time through artist development, media training, finishing schools, and the like. But, as a simple starting point, you can really tap into the concept of having an it factor through this understanding and usage of individualism and tantalization. To be successful, however, your individualism must have clear definition, and you must express it confidently. Any confusion within yourself will confuse your audience. You also must embrace the concept of tantalization so that you can emerge from obscurity and make an impression on others. No one will know that you have baked a pie until they can smell it! As you pursue fame, your it factor will help to clean up any misconceptions about who you are and perhaps more importantly, who you are not. In the process, it will also grant a certain level of legitimacy to your stardom. It will enhance the idea that you are born to do what you do. The likeability generated by your it factor can be a wonderfully positive experience, but beware. For every sunshine, there is rain. You see, there will be times when it seems that everybody likes you, but there will also be times when it seems that everyone hates you...

8

YAY! EVERYBODY HATES YOU!

Life in general has its share of unfortunate events, but the famous life is riddled with turmoil. Most people think of the positive attention they will receive in the spotlight, but the negative attention will be quite prevalent as well. Whether you are offending someone in the form of a scandal, or someone is offending you in the form of a scam, it is important to quickly identify these kinds of negative events and take control of the situation as soon as possible. Unfortunately, as a celebrity, people will be waiting for you to fail, even making a living off of your misfortune. And the sad truth is that **as your star becomes brighter, the target on your back becomes bigger**.

Avoidance is a good tactic in regards to potentially damaging situations, but when you still find yourself in some trouble, you will need to address the issues in a manner which turns things back in your favor. With the help of a knowledgeable public relations person and the creative use of spin, you can do just that. So, in this chapter, we will discuss how to navigate through a disruptive scandal, how to use a positive perspective and spin to improve the appearance of your situation, and lastly, how to recognize 10 of the most common scams others will use to sabotage your fame. You can never really anticipate all of life's surprisingly negative experiences, but with some discernment, you can hopefully formulate a game plan that will help you avoid trouble or at least endure unexpected pitfalls.

SCANDAL

A scandal is usually a negative incident that offends the public at large and causes outrage. From the outside looking in, a scandal is disastrous. It shows that you are an immoral, disgraceful person and ruins your career forever. Right? Wrong. From the inside looking out, a scandal is actually a prime opportunity that you can take advantage of, and in the next few paragraphs you will see why. But, let's first take a look at your life prior to a scandal. That will greatly impact your response, the response of others, and possibly the outcome of events.

Whether you like scandal or not, it is part of life in the spotlight, and it never goes away even when you try to avoid it. The higher you go in fame, the more prone you are to the extremes of life, and that includes scandal. Still, there is nothing wrong with attempting to avoid scandal, and scandal is not absolutely necessary for your career. Be the best you can be. **You are not perfect, and even if you were, someone would still hate you**. You are going to mess up, so just be prepared for it. Nevertheless, you can make efforts to build up a positive reputation. A good reputation is credibility developed with people over time by exhibiting positive qualities consistently. This creates what Covey calls an "emotional bank account" with your fans.[1] When your emotional bank account is full, a scandal might cause you to lose a few dollars, but it won't bankrupt you. Casual fans may turn away, but your core will remain. With a strong emotional bank account, people will think more of you and less of the scandal. They will discredit the rumors and the gossip, defend you, and support you. Either way, a planned course of action will help you navigate the treacherous waters of scandal, and you can make it through without losing everything.

When scandal occurs, it is important to stay calm and rational. It is not the end of your career. It is not the end of the world. Despite my awesome chapter title, the idea that everyone hates you is a hasty generalization more fitting for hormonal teenagers. Someone somewhere will still like you, and at no point will everyone hate you. In fact, scandal can actually be used to your benefit because it is the ultimate attention grabber that can make your situation a premier story overnight. In fact, that is why scandal is at the heart of television. Soap operas, reality shows, and saucy dramas rule the airwaves as the scandal element draws in viewers. Now, I'm sure that you would rather be famous than infamous, but the end result from both is becoming well-known. So, if you can suffer through scandal's temporary embarrassment, you can grow from it, emerging stronger. As the saying goes, "any publicity is good publicity." The effects of scandal, however, are widespread, and it can disrupt both your private and public life. Different components of the scandal recovery will also need to be addressed in both realms so that you can rebound most effectively. It will take a great deal of individual strength and some tactical maneuvering on your part, but a good scandal could become the very platform you need to extend your fame and fulfill deeper positive purposes. To do this, you will need to implement Operation 7-11.

As you can see in Figure 8-1, Operation 7-11 is a protocol that I have developed for handling a scandal in public and private simultaneously. The name alludes to the 7 public steps you take coupled with 11 private steps. The private steps include all the public steps, just at different times.

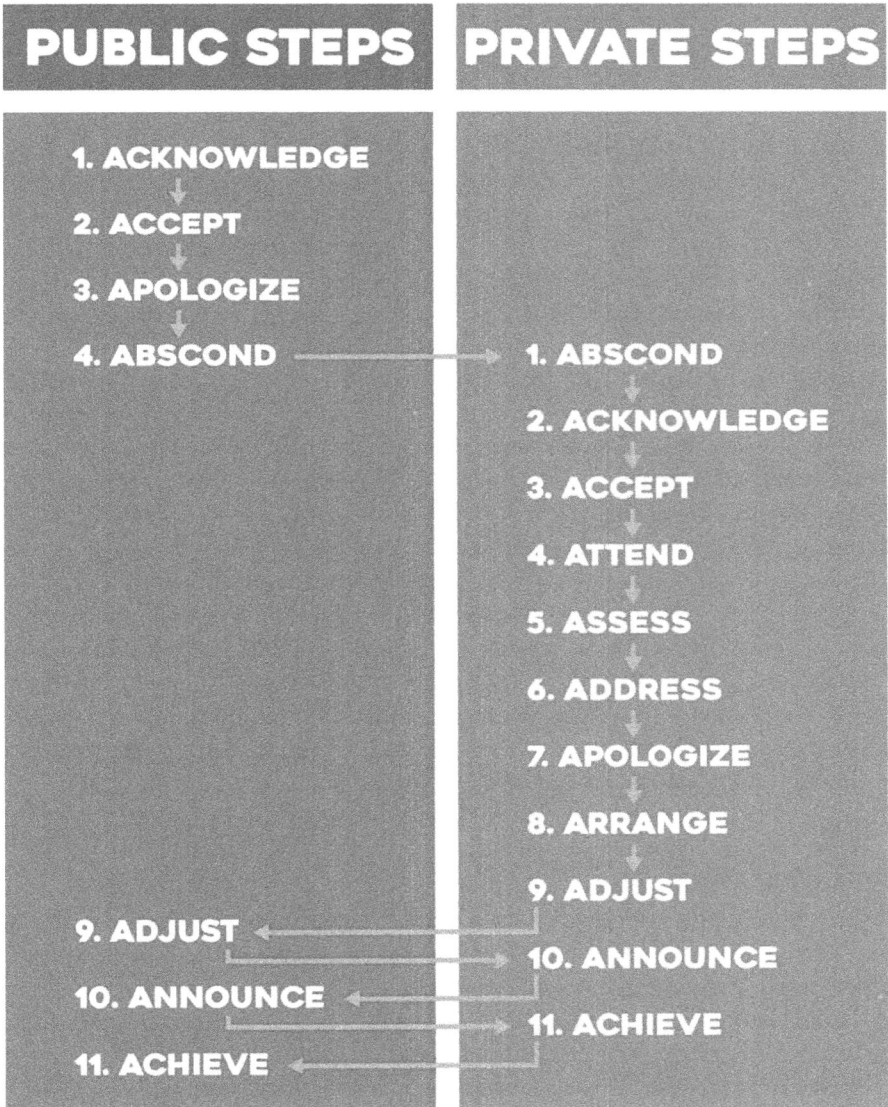

OPERATION

7-11

PUBLIC STEPS | PRIVATE STEPS

PUBLIC STEPS

1. ACKNOWLEDGE
2. ACCEPT
3. APOLOGIZE
4. ABSCOND

9. ADJUST
10. ANNOUNCE
11. ACHIEVE

PRIVATE STEPS

1. ABSCOND
2. ACKNOWLEDGE
3. ACCEPT
4. ATTEND
5. ASSESS
6. ADDRESS
7. APOLOGIZE
8. ARRANGE
9. ADJUST
10. ANNOUNCE
11. ACHIEVE

Figure 8-1

However, the private steps are also more detailed as they include four additional actions. This method of recovery from scandal can be compared to the painting of a portrait. **The public part of scandal recovery uses broad brushes while the private issues require finer, more delicate strokes**.

There is also a specific order to the Operation 7-11 diagram. On the public side, acknowledgement, acceptance, and apology come first, whether those matters have been addressed privately or not. Next comes absconding, simultaneously in the public and private life. All of your private issues are dealt with at that time, and none of the actions that occur in the private sector are necessary knowledge for the public until you get towards the end. Finally, as you adjust, announce, and achieve, you then want to relay each of those successes to the public each time you accomplish one of them. So now, let's take a look at how each step contributes to your scandal recovery. If you follow this plan, all your failing *F*'s will be turned into straight *A*'s!

ACKNOWLEDGE (PUBLICLY)

The first step in scandal recovery is to acknowledge what happened. Doing this prevents the public from accusing you of being in denial and impedes the flow of unsubstantiated gossip by opening the door for your side of the story. The best way to acknowledge is at one comprehensive gathering. **A single word from a single source at a single time will leave little room for double-talk or misinterpretations**. Depending on your situation, your gathering may be in the form a press conference, a town hall meeting, a board meeting, or a family discussion. In any event, make sure to gather all the facts and get your story straight. Lies and inconsistencies at this moment will make you look suspicious, especially if contrary information surfaces later on, so speak with surety. Do not speak on anything you don't know or are unsure about, and don't feel obligated to answer every single question at this time. This does not, however, mean that you should ignore questions. Instead, just decline to speak on certain matters until further knowledge is available. Acknowledgement is the first line of defense against the wildfire of scandal, so quickly erect this crucial barrier before things get out of control.

ACCEPT (PUBLICLY)

Next, there are two things that you should accept publicly: the magnitude of the scandal and your role in the scandal. A primary natural reaction is to minimize the events with the hope of drawing less negativity; however, in doing so, you run the risk of appearing uncaring and apathetic regarding the situation. This will cause your fans to view you as guilty, cold-blooded, insincere, immature, or arrogant. Instead, be as serious as possible and relay the gravity of the situation and your personal concern even if it seems like small potatoes to you.

The other natural response is to blame other people. You may do well to acknowledge the situation, but finger-pointing from the start can be a fear-induced attempt to shift focus away from you. This is not the time to talk about everyone else. This is the time to talk about you. What role did you play, if any? Why are you being associated? Even if you are innocent of the accusations, do not become overly defensive; let others defend you. This step is not about innocence; it's about involvement. Show that you are concerned about what happened and that you are aware of your inclusion despite validity. Then, the public will take you seriously and be less inclined to believe that you are brushing the matter off or playing the blame game.

APOLOGIZE (PUBLICLY)

In today's scandal-driven world, the public apology is probably the most iconic and memorable moment of the scandal. Here, you need to be either very sincere or very good at acting. The pregnant pauses and crocodile tears need to flow as you show remorse for your actions. If you were uninvolved and do not need to apologize, at least show that you are concerned about the negative circumstances, the other people affected, and your unjust victimiza-tion. The apology is probably the biggest and hardest step, but it is absolutely necessary. Forgiveness may not be returned if an apology is not given first. Still, most people do not want you down and out forever, especially if you are valuable to the community, and especially in America where media has pro-grammed us for decades with comeback stories. Most will want to see you back on top, but the road to redemption starts with an apology. If you are not dramatic, your apology does not have to be drawn-out. Instead, make a quick, sincere, heart-felt apology immediately, and the public may soon be back on your side.

ABSCOND (PUBLICLY)

After the first three steps have been completed, usually all at once during a single press conference, you should make like a tree and get out of there! (I'm sorry, that was for all of the *Back To The Future* fans). But seriously, if you lay low at this point, it will make you less susceptible to continued scrutiny, per-sonal attack, and hounding reporters looking for a new angle. The people who stay in the spotlight during scandal usually continue to be picked on, because they are still constantly in the eyes and ears, and thus the minds of the public. **A scandal is like an unquenchable fire, so don't stand there and try to be a firefighter**. You cannot throw water onto the fire of scandal and expect it to be put out. You must let it die out slowly on its own. And, the best way to do that is to be forgotten for a while. Just like fame, infamy dies without attention. **When you disappear, distraction will diminish your debacle.**

ACKNOWLEDGE (PRIVATELY)

One you abscond, taking a moment away from the spotlight, you will be able to see things a bit more clearly. The step of acknowledgement is repeated in the private realm along with a couple of other steps, but don't think redundancy, think reality. The public acknowledgement is a broad overview to appease others, whether you have reached a true state of acknowledgement or not. The private acknowledgement, however, is a genuine personal reflection in which you disregard pressure from others and examine the details of the situation. If you acknowledge something in public that you ignore in private, it shows a certain callousness and serious denial issues on your part. If this is the case, you lead a double life, and your public and private entities are harmfully disconnected. If you do not acknowledge, you run the risk of making the same mistake over again by not addressing the current issue, and the public will be much less forgiving if they feel that they were duped the first time around. The strong desire for the way things used to be can compel you to pretend like your scandal did not happen, but private acknowledgement will set you up for a healthy recovery process and a strong return to the spotlight, so do not fear the journey.

ACCEPT (PRIVATELY)

With private acceptance, you see the matter through your own eyes, not the eyes of the public. Here, you cut through the facade and become completely honest with yourself, enduring all the associated emotions. This important step determines how you will handle the problem from here on out. Ask yourself the important questions and develop your personal viewpoint on the magnitude of events and the role you played. Is this a trivial issue played up by the media, or did you do something seriously damaging to yourself, to your career, to your family and friends, or to society at large? Were you heavily involved, or are you being unfairly associated? The scandal might be a big deal in your public address, but actually a small matter in your personal life, or vice versa. Your mind can clear, and your perspective can change when you are out of the spotlight, so this is why absconding is necessary.

ATTEND (PRIVATELY)

Once you have clearly identified the issues, it is time for you to attend to yourself. You cannot continue business as usual and expect recovery. Instead, you need to reconfigure your life priorities so that your focus is shifted onto yourself and off other people, things, and events. When you abscond, you are not hiding from work, you are working on yourself. To the outsider looking in, you are just doing nothing and waiting for things to blow over. But in actuality, you are making a concerted effort to shift the focus from what you do to who you are.

ASSESS (PRIVATELY)

The assessment step is an evaluation of yourself in relation to your current situation. It is a return to your tree of stable stardom, specifically your roots of regulation. At this time, determine whether or not your actions lined up with your core identity and principles. If you find yourself to be at fault, allow yourself to grieve, to feel awful, to have a pity party. These feelings are natural, you are out of the spotlight, and you should let your emotions and reactions flow freely. Remember, however, that you are not alone. Countless people, famous or not, have been caught up in situations that they regret. Detail what you did wrong, try to figure out why you did it, and prepare to move forward.

ADDRESS (PRIVATELY)

When you address the issue privately, that is when you roll up your sleeves and dive into the process of change. This process is most effective when supporters are involved. **Don't try to change yourself by yourself**. You may be too weak to handle things on your own, but there is strength in numbers. Addressing the scandal privately may include going to rehab, attending therapy sessions, speaking with clergy or other mentors, researching your situation, and more. Once you speak with others, you may find that they have different takes on various steps in your process, some of which you may have already covered. Don't brush off these critiques. The perspective of supporters during times like these is invaluable. Although you may want to rush through this part, don't try to speed up the process. This is open-life surgery; it will take time and dedication.

APOLOGIZE (PRIVATELY)

After everything has been addressed, that is when you can most sincerely and effectively apologize to the people you have hurt. By this point, you should know what you did, why you did it, why you won't do it again, and the steps you are taking to prevent a reoccurrence. At this stage, you should view yourself as a changed person, officially on the other side of your situation. If others don't forgive you, that is their issue. Your hands are clean, and you should proceed accordingly. This step, however, is not just about others. Long after an incident has occurred, the scandal can haunt your memories and plague your psyche. As silly as it may seem, you may very well need to issue yourself an apology and forgive yourself as well. That way, you will no longer carry the weight of this problem either. If you compare this step with your initial apology, you will be amazed at the level of sincerity and genuineness that your new-found revelation and awareness will bring about.

ARRANGE (PRIVATELY)

Once you have addressed your issues, you will be excited to arrange or rearrange your life. During this step, you will begin making plans that answer key questions. How do you intend to bounce back from this? What messages will you continue to convey to the public? What changes will be made to avoid these kinds of situations in the future? Who will attest to your recovery? As symbols of your rehabilitation, you could do charity work, make public service announcements, become involved in mentorship programs, make charitable donations, become a motivational speaker, write a helpful book, and more. Take the knowledge that you have gained from others and from your own experience and formulate a plan that demonstrates recovery, growth, and an ability to shine even brighter in the spotlight when given the opportunity.

ADJUST (PRIVATELY)

This is the part where you implement change in your life. Quietly execute the plans that regard your personal life and your inner circle. Inform those close to you of your intentions so that there is no confusion once you are back in the light. Don't skip this step, get anxious, and jump back into the public's scrutiny just yet. Do something on a private level and see how it is perceived. If your change is incomplete, if you slip up one time, even if you look like you're thinking about possibly doing something wrong, the public will be raring to crucify you all over again. Remember, the outsiders will not have seen any of your growth, so expect doubt. Structure your changes in a way that goes above and beyond in order to convince unbelievers of your transformation.

ADJUST (PUBLICLY)

At this point, your period of absconding is over. You are back onto the public scene, but it still may not be a fanfare quite yet. You have been out of the picture for a while, and this step just reminds the public of you and your situation. Here, you share major adjustments or improvements that you have made, gaining even more of their confidence and trust since your public apology. Remember, from the public's point of view, you have seemingly gone from apology to adjustment overnight. That is the power of absconding which will amaze people and cause them to think even more highly of you.

Some people will still be doubtful, but their numbers will decrease if you remain consistent in your message and actions. You are no longer a dog with his tail tucked between his legs. You are now a great person who has overcome adversity.

ANNOUNCE (PRIVATELY)

Now that your image is restored, it is time to start using it. Don't let your fame die with a scandal. Don't ever give up on yourself. Remain in the company of encouraging people. A scandal is not an excuse for failure. Pick yourself up, dust yourself off, and get back to work. Depending on the length of your absconding and the level of your fame, people will be impatiently waiting for you to return to what made you famous. Here, you announce the fame-related portions of your plans to everyone in your camp before you release it to the world. However, don't come back with the same old routine; do something new and exciting that will show growth, increase zeal, and propel you back into the spotlight with fury.

ANNOUNCE (PUBLICLY)

Tell the public the big things you have in store. Most have been waiting for a comeback, so let them know that the time is now. Some will never forgive and never let go, but don't let them negatively affect your disposition and send you backwards. Try not to answer any more questions about the past. The past is past at last. Get everyone thinking about the future, but if someone keeps probing, don't become angry. Show that you are comfortable making fun of yourself if you did something stupid. The comfort level with which you speak during these moments show whether or not you have really grown.

ACHIEVE (PRIVATELY)

I have included this step of private achievement as a cautionary approach, because the last thing you want to do is get out there and flop. Your transformation will be more appealing if growth occurs in all areas of your life. Figure out a way to profit from your hardship and show that you have the enhanced vitality to accomplish. "Metabolize pain as energy."[2] Go through trial and error. Test and retest. Obtain advice from your counsel. Make sure you are going to wow the public.

ACHIEVE (PUBLICLY)

Get out there and do your thing! It's as simple as that. Hopefully you will feel refreshed, renewed, and re-energized.

SPIN

For the Scandal

When you talk about scandal, the first thought for any public relations person on your team is damage control. They will understandably want to do everything possible to prevent things from becoming worse. This is primarily accomplished by controlling information. Your public relations team may withhold information, present new information, remove you from the public or from a certain environment, have others speak on your behalf, create counter messages, and more. However, a particularly interesting and effective tactic called spin goes beyond information control and attempts to control people's perception of such information.

Spin can be described as "the activity of trying to control the way something is described to the public in order to influence what people think about it."[3] For example, if you asked for a healthy balanced meal, and I promised you something with fruits, vegetables, meat, dairy, and grains, you would probably be pleased with the offer, but when I bring you a greasy ham and pineapple pizza, you might have second thoughts. Why? Because I used spin to present the information. So, you perceived my offer in the most favorable light. Notice that I did not lie to you. The pizza contains all the food group elements in some form and is healthy on some level, but it is probably not what you had in mind. Now, if you feel duped, your emotions are completely justified. Spin lives in varying shades of gray, and one can even put a spin on spin! Some view spin as creative presentation of information while others see it as deceptive and manipulative; either way, it works.

If you are caught up in a scandal, spin can be very helpful when information control is impossible or ineffective. If you don't have a good public relations person, I suggest getting one when involved in a public predicament. They are professionals at smoothing over your rough edges, and you can often make matters worse by trying to handle things on your own. Remember, however, that spin's usage is broad. With it, you can creatively present facts or tell flat-out lies. Your core will determine which road you are most comfortable traveling. Spin is also not always an automatic fix-it formula. If people don't buy what you're selling, your damage control can easily backfire. Your perspective on the perspectives of others must be keen, and your foundation must be rock solid in order to effectively navigate the troubling waters of scandal, especially in its crucial initial stages. Spin can be an adequate plug for a leaky ship, but don't rely on it to get you all the way to shore. **The cold hard truth can surprisingly draw the warmest sympathies**.

For the Setup

A scandal can ironically be an attractive measure because it creates controversy that ultimately gets people talking about you and/or your situation. As we just discussed, the ability to manipulate people's perception of an event can be powerful; however, the ability to manipulate the actual events can be a lucrative setup from the start that offers even more control. With this in mind, not everyone avoids controversy like the plague. In fact, some appear to relish it, and those people are called publicists.

The art of publicity in America dates back to the mid-1800s with P.T. Barnum, who is most known for the traveling circus that still carries his name today. However, when his circus was in town, he often also turned the town into a circus in order to draw attention to his attraction. Barnum fabricated biographies, sent letters to the press from imaginary fans, and defended himself against fake accusers.[4] Today, you only need to pick up the latest gossip magazine to see how the need to be noticed has resulted in more extreme antics. Criminal offenses, sexcapades, pregnancies and abortions, animals, children, politics, money, marriages and divorces, rehab stints, and even deaths are all used today as elements which one can spin into fantastic stories to get attention.

Publicity has evolved over the years, but the perpetually increasing need to garner attention is ever-present in fame yet elusive in fulfillment. This occurs because we live in an age where the constant bombardment of information seems to always provide distraction. "As journalist Keith Altham observed, 'It seems ridiculous in retrospect, but gimmicks were necessary early on for publicity. You first have to grab the attention of the media before anyone will notice you.'"[5] Exposure, however, is a two-way street, and negative events can seemingly shut you down before you really get started. Still, publicity stunts have propelled many stars into the spotlight, and the use of created controversy can be the difference between just being talented or being talked-about.

The media, and by association, the corporations that run them are the gatekeepers to widespread fame because they have the most resources to reach the most people. So typically, to reach the highest levels of fame, you have to play by their rules which today involves sensationalism, shock value, and negativity. Although the occasional "feel-good" story is thrown into the mix from time to time, when it comes to publicity stunts, gimmicks, and various other ploys to get attention and thus fame, ethics and morality tend to fly out of the window pretty quickly.

It's no secret that negativity gets attention while good goes virtually unnoticed. If you doubt that, then just watch the news. Most of the featured news stories will be about negative events, because those kinds of stories will bring them the most ratings in a fiercely competitive industry. Strangely, it is not the celebrity's successes but their flaws which humanize them in our eyes and enable us to relate to them. "The true hero is flawed…A hero without flaw is of no interest to an audience or to the universe, which after all is based on conflict and opposition."[6] Publicists and other handlers may want you to be controversial, risqué, different, daring, or dangerous, even if that doesn't fit your true personality. If you are too good, too nice, too perfect, too normal, or too stable, it could actually hurt your fame by making you too boring. Expect to make some identity decisions in this regard early on. Will you stay steadfast to a particular moral identity? Will you turn a blind eye to the tactics of your publicist? Will you view your public persona as a character that does not reflect you personally? Or will you have an anything goes attitude, be willing to do anything for fame, and become the catastrophe that people crave? This may seem blunt, but let's face it, people love a train wreck.

SCAMS

There are many ways to get noticed, but hopefully you will set the boundaries for yourself that will promote fame, not infamy. Still, a life in the spotlight is such an incredibly captivating notion that most people will do just about anything to get it these days. Especially with the advent of sensational reality shows and contests where ordinary people become household names seemingly overnight, the public is inspired to leap blindly into the various avenues to stardom. And, why not? It looks so easy on TV. However, the flipside to that desperate pursuit is a stunning degree of vulnerability. When people will do just about anything to get something, scammers are sure to be lurking around.

Scammers are people who use deception or fraud to swindle you. They can get you caught up in over half of the troubles listed in the perils of fame, so it is important to watch out for them and understand how their traps work. The entertainment industry is notorious for scammers who prey on the bright-eyed, bushy-tailed Hollywood newcomers before they are aware of what roads they should take. After spending over a decade in the entertainment industry, I have fallen into my fair share of traps, and I have found 10 major signs that may indicate a scam. Hopefully you can learn from them and not make the same mistakes that countless other have made.

Upfront Money

Asking for money upfront is probably the most well-known tactic of scammers. You should act very cautiously with anyone who approaches you in this way, especially if it seems like an unreasonably large sum of money. Sure, money is essential to fame-building, but many other factors will need to contribute to your success. If you depend solely on your money to make you famous, your money will become famous before you do.

When I first started doing hip hop music, I signed up for a showcase in San Francisco that promised exposure to record labels. My band and I blindly paid the upfront fee without researching the event or the producing company. We rented a car and drove several hours to San Francisco and back. At the end of the day, there were no significant industry people present, and that experience did absolutely nothing for our careers. Even before the event began, I was starting to think that we had been scammed. But, I was so eager for an opportunity that it clouded my judgment. **Before you give money, get knowledge**. Every dollar you put towards your fame is an investment, so expect a return.

Contract Issues

Problematic contracts or the lack thereof is another warning sign that you may be in a bad situation. When it comes to fame, the more you have in writing, the better. If someone that you are in partnership with is leery of a written agreement, then you should be leery of them. A contract pressures everyone involved to guarantee a certain level of integrity. It stops people from saying one thing and doing another. However, a short, vague, or poorly written contract can be just as bad as no contract at all. Contract details also depend on your particular situation. I have signed adequate one page contracts, and I have reviewed major label contracts over 100 pages in length. Even so, when it comes to a significant matter, I'll take a 100-page contract over a 1-page agreement any day.

Also, be wary of long term contracts that tie you down for a considerable amount of time, or exclusive contracts which tie you down to the entity you have contracted with. Long-term deals can be difficult to get out of if things go sour, and if your contract is exclusive, you may not be allowed to work with anyone else. If necessary, also have a lawyer look over each deal. Even when all the significant deal points are present, a lawyer's take on language and interpretation can be invaluable. You can really lose big with contractual errors, so learn about standard contract elements and compare the contracts you receive with sample contracts. A little boredom at the beginning will be much better than a headache at the end.

Contracts have been a thorn in my side ever since I started doing music professionally. I have worked in such casual circles that contracting has seemed unnecessary. Yet, people have owed me thousands of dollars because I did not write or enforce their contractual obligation. I amicably operated on handshake agreements, and when it came time to pay up, my money was nowhere in sight. Now, to protect myself, I have written my own contracts for just about any situation. I even have close friends sign them if they want to use my services.

Temporal Pressure

Temporal pressure occurs when someone urges you to act quickly. Time constraints are normal because no one wants a deal or negotiation to drag on for too long, but when time seems to be more important than a quality deal that all parties are satisfied with, there may be just cause for suspicion. Anyone who wants you to act in an unreasonably short amount of time is trying to get you to act impulsively without any critical thinking. Don't let anyone do this to you. There is a difference between choosing a candy bar at the supermarket checkout line and making a life decision in regards to your fame.

A few years ago, I was presented with a management representation contract. The lady who offered it spoke with me only via the internet, never over the phone or in person. That alone was suspicious. She also gave me a strict time limit on signing the deal and stated that it would no longer be offered if I did not sign by the deadline. I was seeking management at the time and had never had this kind of formal offer before. An irrational side of me wanted to sign, just so I could say that I had a management deal. But, the manager's aloofness along with the temporal restrictions was really off-putting. So, I declined the offer. Additionally, the contract was poorly written, and I never would have agreed to it anyway without some major alterations. I was disappointed at the time, but since then I have rethought my need for management. I have gone in some different directions, and I am glad that I did not get locked into a bad deal by succumbing to the temporal pressure.

By no means am I saying that you should never act quickly. Very often in fame an amazing yet extremely time-sensitive opportunity presents itself, and you have to make the call. But the fact that these types of situations do occur often makes the scam that much more deceptive. You should be equally capable of making quick decisions under the right circumstances, but an appropriate amount of allotted time is always an asset to you.

Delusory Promises

Beware of people who make extraordinary promises to you and inflate your ego. Fame has a fantastical element to it, and if you are desperate for the spotlight, a scammer can flatter you into believing that your imaginary world of fame is reality. But, when you are high on yourself and the illusion of fame, that is usually when the rug is pulled out from under you. You might want to think twice if someone tells you that they can make you the next

Michael Jackson in six weeks when you have never sung before. That time frame for learning how to sing at an advanced level is unrealistic. That time frame for achieving fame is unrealistic. Remain humble and research your chances of success. Study others who have done what you are trying to do. Then, instead of accepting someone else's propaganda, you will have a realistic idea of your fame potential.

Easy Street

You should expect the pursuit of fame to be a challenging endeavor. It is the challenging road that gives anything in life its worth. The more challenging career pays more. The gem that is more difficult to find is worth more. On the other hand, no one puts grass in a safety deposit box. It grows everywhere, and there is no significant challenge to obtain it, so it is virtually worthless in our eyes. You should view every easy-street scam in the same manner. I'm sure you know the saying: "If it sounds too good to be true, it probably is." Have you noticed that many of the so-called overnight successes seem to disappear overnight as well? But the people who have gradually worked their way into the spotlight have stayed around much longer. According to famous businessman Robert Herjavec, "It takes 10 to 15 years to become an overnight success."[7] Easy street does not allow for the growth and maturity gained by overcoming obstacles on a more challenging path. It sets you up to be ill-prepared to handle the end goal. **Don't look for an open hand. Look for an opportunity to prove yourself**.

Going Nowhere

People who end up in the spotlight rarely get there by accident. You must make a decision early on as to how serious this is to you. Are you going to be a professional or a hobbyist? Those are two different roads with two different goals, yet again in today's reality-competition-TV world, where everyone seems to think they are destined for stardom, the two paths are becoming frustratingly intertwined. Hobby denotes a just-for-fun attitude. It totally conflicts with the seriousness, professionalism, and highly competitive nature of the fame objective. When the hobbyist mentality is mixed in with a strive for fame, there are no career-advancement goals, which means the drive for growth is slowed or nonexistent.

If you are serious about being famous, you should avoid people who say, "We're not concerned about making it big," "This is just for the experience," or "Oh, we're just doing it for the love of…" These are statements from the kinds of people who will go nowhere. I can't tell you how many times I have been dragged into music groups with no goals or plans. At one point, I was in a band that rehearsed for almost two years without ever performing a single show! And even after all that, the group never seemed to get that much better. It was the epitome of Nowheresville. Before you get involved with anyone, determine whether they are a hobbyist or a professional. Do they have specific goals, or are they meandering, hoping that one day they will hit the fame lottery?

No-names

Another way to go nowhere fast is to associate with no-names. I use the term no-name to refer to people who are not well-known and/or have no track record of success. Also, be wary of companies that change their name often, have multiple names, or are totally unfamiliar. These companies can often hide their bad reputation this way. If Company X is exposed as a scam, they may change their name to Company Y and run the same scam until they are found out again. I have seen this often with TV and movie casting agencies and modeling agencies. When you partner with a no-name, it is truly a case of the blind leading the blind. How can someone who has done nothing turn your nothing into something? If you want to be famous, you need to infiltrate the circles of famous people and work your way up. You tend to become like the people you hang around. The people who are famous obviously know how it's done, so you should strive to be in their company and learn from them.

Name-droppers

Name-dropping occurs when you use your association with another famous person to make yourself seem famous. And, if you are working with someone who name-drops excessively, they could very well be a no-name in disguise. I won't harp on name-dropping too much, because well, it works. It is common practice, especially in Hollywood, and it may open doors for you. If I named the famous people I have worked with, you would probably think more highly of me. So why is name-dropping listed here? Well, at the end of the day, bragging about who you know only gets you so far. I refer to fame in this limited manner as associate fame. If fame were a tangible object, associate fame would place another individual or entity between you and it. Yes, you can still become famous that way, but your fame would not be intrinsic, and your connection to fame would be dependent and weaker than a direct connection. If you are a name-dropper thriving on associate fame, you can scam yourself into becoming the shadow artist to which Julia Cameron refers. When you name-drop excessively, you are living in the shadows, not the spotlight.

Has-beens

Has-beens are people who used to have a high level of fame but are no longer very famous. They may try to appear like they are still at the peak of celebrity, but their perceived reality is actually a delusion as fame has long passed them by. You can spot a has-been's characteristics in nearly every aspect of their identity. Their clothes, hair, lingo, philosophies, associates, methods, and more will be painfully dated or out-of-style. These kinds of people may have good bits of advice here and there, but they are not the ones who will advance your career. They will be too busy trying to hold onto every last little thread of theirs. Remember, when it comes to fame, the question is, "What have you done for me lately?" If you are not constantly in the public conscience, you are soon forgotten.

Conflict

The strength of your identity core is very important because your fame constantly challenges it. People or circumstances will continually provide you with opportunities to say or do something which conflicts with your foundation and disregards your conscience. These conscience conflicts are the unseen internal battles that wage beneath the surface of glitz and glamour, plaguing, even tormenting those in the spotlight. They go against your roots of regulation, compromise your person, make you uncomfortable, present themselves as the only route, or even incite fear in you. Submitting to conscience conflicts causes you to do things that go against your values and changes your core. Even if a decision seems insignificant, each little deviation chips away at your identity until one day you wake up and don't know who you are anymore. Evaluate each conflict, great or small, against your roots and determine whether or not you need to reject or accept a change. An occasional identity adjustment will actually prolong your time in the spotlight, but changing with every wind or taking a stone-walled approach to change are unhealthy extremes.

■□■□■□■□

When scandals and scams occur, it is only the end of the world if you allow it to be. Instead, let your goal, your dream, your purpose inspire you to gather your internal and external strengths and fight back once you have been attacked. Don't just stand there and let your career be damaged. The same creative power that made you a star will be the same creativity that will enable you to sustain despite scandal or sidestep a scam. Additionally, any story headlines that you purposely create for attention will survive in relation to your creative ability to peak public interest and captivate amidst a world of distraction. Perfection is impossible, the appearance of perfection is boring, and constant negativity is repellant, but a little bit of controversy draws attention that can always be used to your advantage. Negative situations like anything else in fame will come and go, but your response to these kinds of events will be the constant that is more important than the events themselves.

Works Cited

1 (Covey 188)

2 (Cameron 135)

3 ("Spin Control")

4 (Borkowski 22-25)

5 (Cross 167)

6 (Stein 135)

7 ("Episode 307")

9
THE MERCHANT MENTALITY

During their journeys, fame seekers are often surprised and unprepared when hit with the stark reality that the fame game isn't much of a game at all at higher levels. It's business…big business. We see the organism, the person who attracts us as fans, but behind the organism is an organization that provides the resources for that organism to produce on a large scale. Whether you work with an established company, start your own business, or both, a familiarity with general business concepts will be empowering for you.

Now, you don't have to become a business law specialist or a marketing guru, but some fundamental aspects of business in today's world will enable you to function efficiently and progress quicker in your fame endeavors. We have already discussed the essentials of understanding yourself and others, so the conceptual translation to business should be fairly easy. Since organizations are composed of organisms, they operate in a similar manner.

When I came to California I made the wise decision of going to college and majoring in music industry, not music. I had the talent, but I had no business understanding or experience. After learning quite a bit about business in general and about nearly every job in the music industry as well, today I enjoy working both onstage and offstage. Being both creatively driven and business-minded is rare, so I expect many of you with dreams of being in the spotlight to be turned off by a business section that highlights what happens behind the scenes. You may ask, "Why can't I just hire someone to do all of the business stuff for me?" And, my response is that you can, and you should! However, there are a few issues that come along with hiring outside business help, and at least a general knowledge of business will prevent you from becoming trapped in a bad situation.

First, if you are just starting out, it may be difficult to afford business people. Many may also be unwilling to take on someone new and unproven. Handling initial business aspects on your own will prevent you from stagnating and enable you to understand yourself more while establishing a track record that will encourage other organisms and organizations to work with you. Secondly, getting someone to do something for you without understanding what they are doing is a perfect setup for them to take advantage of you. If you are not business-minded from the start, you lose control of your fame. The people you hire control it for you, and that is a step on the path to becoming an out-of-control celebrity. Without business knowledge, you can easily go from having full command of your life to becoming a puppet and not knowing what's going on anymore.

Business can be complex and there may be some aspects you are drawn to more than others, but having at least some knowledge will give you more understanding, more leveraging ability, and more of a sense of command over your career. In the following pages, we will look at 11 major business components and their relation to the fame industry.

STRUCTURE

There are four major business structures: sole proprietorship, general partnership, limited liability company (LLC), and corporation. Other variations exist, but these four are fundamental for understanding, with LLC's being the newest addition. Each type of business is different, and your structure of choice will depend on your specific needs and desires. Basic summaries and opinions of these four structures are outlined in this first section, and the rest of this chapter is meant to serve as an introduction to important areas of business that specifically concern someone in the spotlight. If you feel weak in any business component, I encourage you to go beyond this chapter and learn more so that you can make informed business decisions.

Sole Proprietorship

The most popular and introductory business form is the sole proprietorship. With this business type, the business is very attached to its owner and is not a separate entity. In addition to owning and operating, you are also personally responsible for all business debts. This structure works well for those in the spotlight, because essentially, you are the business. Sole proprietorships are simple to setup and operate. In fact, they are so simple that once you collect money for your product or service offering, you have started a sole proprietorship and may be taxed accordingly, whether you realize it or not! To begin a sole proprietorship, you simply must register your name and obtain any license you may need to operate. Your personal name can be the name of the business, or you can obtain a DBA (Doing Business As) license and operate under a fictitious business name. The difference would be Joe Blow or Joe Blow's Movie Set Design. As you can see, the DBA name can establish legitimacy and help new customers quickly identify what you do.

My first business was a sole proprietorship, and I recommend it as a starter business structure for anyone new to the spotlight. I made my own hours, I kept simple financial records, and it worked well for me for 5 years until I wanted to change it. There is no special accounting required for sole proprietorships, and business taxes may be filed together with any other personal taxes. In addition, sole proprietorships qualify for several tax deductions on many of the items that you may use for business purposes. This may include home office usage, business mileage and other car expenses, performance attire, business meals, equipment, office supplies, bank fees, startup costs, registration fees, rentals, and more. The sole proprietorship is the oldest form of business, and the ease of operation will allow you to equally pursue your creative endeavors. You will also gain fundamental knowledge and experience that will help you in more complicated businesses later on.

Partnership

When you form a business with another person or a group of people, you have started a partnership. A partnership is similar to a sole proprietorship in that when you start doing business, you have essentially formed the business. Once you and your bandmates decide to record an album or play a show together, you have formed a partnership. Even without paperwork, it can be formed on a verbal or handshake deal and hold up in a court of law. So, when starting this form of business, it is a good idea to draft a detailed agreement. This may prevent the biggest downfall of all partnerships: dispute amongst the partners. With regards to liability, all owners are typically responsible for business debts in a partnership; however, limited partnerships and limited liability partnerships can reduce owner liability. Just like sole proprietorships, partnerships are not considered separate entities, so income is taxed on each partner's individual tax return. Partnerships are also eligible for the same favorable tax deductions.

I have never tried or liked the idea of a partnership, because I have rarely found partners who share my vision and work ethic. Even in school, I hated group assignments. I would have to do all the work just so I could receive a decent grade, while everyone else slacked off. Now, I'm not saying a partnership can't work. Two heads are better than one, and two or more people can exponentially increase your efforts. Just always be cautious when putting your fame in the hands of others.

LLC

An LLC or limited liability company is a middle ground business structure that provides the liability protection of a corporation and perpetual existence, but with the option to be taxed as a sole proprietorship or a partnership. It's like wearing business casual attire; it makes you look good, but at the same time, you feel comfortable. LLC's are the newest type of business structure; however, they already exist in several augmentations. An LLC can be managed by a single member like the sole proprietorship, by multiple members like the partnership, or by managers like a corporation. Unlike the sole proprietorship or partnership, the LLC remains a separate entity from the owner in each case. Additionally, some of the business formalities associated with the LLC can be as simple or complex as desired. On the other hand, there are a few disadvantages. In addition to hefty annual filing fees in many states, LLC's also require articles of organization and annual reports in some places. An LLC is also not appropriate for public offering, and even angel investors and venture capitalists prefer to invest in a corporation. Despite the negatives, the unprecedented flexibility of the LLC is naturally causing it to grow in popularity, and I would also recommend it for anyone pursuing a life in the spotlight.

Corporation

The corporation like the LLC is a separate entity with perpetual existence; however, it is owned by shareholders, managed by directors, and operated by officers. The big upside to the corporation is the ability to procure capital investment from shareholders. This enables corporations to become the powerful financial juggernauts of the business world. Corporations, though, require a great deal of administrative attention, and I don't recommend this at all for any of the fresh faces of fame. In addition to annual filing fees and periodic reporting, your corporation will need to have formal voting, required meetings, and specific tabulation of meeting minutes. Also, corporations require several staff members and infrastructure to accomplish requirements and meet the expectations of the shareholders. Running a corporation takes away precious time that you could commit to honing your craft and sharpening your skill sets. A corporation also seems to make you either less of an owner and more of a product or vice versa. The delicate balance between both is extremely difficult to achieve in this structure.

Still, business formation is part of the protections of fame, and a corporation is the ultimate insulation from angry fans who want to sue you and a government that wants its share in taxes. Once incorporated, your personal assets are more protected, and your liability is usually only limited to your investment in the corporation. If you have the time and personnel to deal with the requirements of a corporation, significant assets to protect, and large sums of money, incorporation may still be the right road for you. Many celebrities do incorporate themselves, and that is a viable option as well if you have reached an operating plateau that justifies it.

Restriction vs. Reward

When considering these business entities, most people think about risk and reward. But, for someone who wants to be in the spotlight, your thoughts should also include a restriction-reward deliberation. If you view each of the business forms on a sliding scale, you will see an increase in the potential reward (profit) as you move from a sole proprietorship to a corporation. However, on that same scale there are increasing degrees of personal limitation as you move to the more complex businesses. For example, if you have your heart set on being signed to a major record label, then throw your identity in the trash and be prepared to become what *they* want you to become. You will be told what to say, what to sing, where to go, how to dress, and possibly more. Why? Because all major record labels are now owned by large corporations. And, corporations are beholden to shareholders. Thus, there is intense pressure to make immediate profit. So, if the way you walk, talk, or sing doesn't turn into dollars, they will not sign you. Have you ever wondered why music today tends to all sound the same? You hear the same songs over and over from the same handful of bands because it's corporate radio. Radio today is simplified music for the masses with profit maximization as the chief goal. **Today's media are houses of advertising with doors made of entertainment**.

Now, it's not my intention to completely bash corporations because they do allow for maximum provisioning, profit, and proliferation. They can propel your fame, but it comes at a price, and I'm just showing you that price. Corporations have a rigid cookie-cutter mentality, and if you don't fit the mold, you will not be accepted. Do you see how that fights against your individuality? What price are you willing to pay for the power of a corporation?

PLANNING

It is amazing to see how many people jump into the spotlight with no plan at all. They expect things to just happen when they arrive, but that is not how it works. Usually initial fame and definitely extended fame are the results of a master plan. And in order to achieve your specific goals, you need to have specific plans. "I want to be famous," is a very bad, nondescript goal. If you are really serious about your fame, you need to make a plan that is specific to you and your particular situation. Despite what you see on television, most people rarely become famous overnight. What you see is just the end of a long, arduous process. With today's technological advances and economic instability, more and more gatekeepers to fame are expecting you to show success on a small-scale before they invest in you. Clearly outline your goal and create a specific plan, and you will greatly increase your chances of success.

If you really want to paint a realistic detailed picture of what you are about to do, then I challenge you to write a business plan for your fame. The journey of writing it alone will bring about some stark realizations about yourself, your goals, your resources, and your environment. I would like to say that writing a business plan is not as hard as it seems, but it is truly a laborious process, which is why most people don't do it. However, its purpose is simple. When you are done, your business plan should be able to answer any questions regarding your fame. So, you want to be famous. For what? For how long? What does famous mean for you, and when will you have achieved it? Who is going to help you get there? Who is likely to hold you back? What are you willing to sacrifice? Why will people even pay attention to you? Who are your competitors? How much money will you need to raise to begin your fame? How much money will you need to make to support your fame? The more answers you have to these questions, the better chance you have of being taken seriously and achieving your fame goals. Arbitrary goals may never be realized, but when connected to detailed plans, they are more likely to be accomplished.

CAPITAL

The primary cause of business failure is lack of money or capital, and your fame is no different. Have you noticed that riches and fame seem to go hand in hand? They both feed off each other, and there is obviously a connection. How many famous people can you name that have never been rich as well? As Mark Borkowski notes in *The Fame Game*, even in the early stages of Hollywood, publicists would grease the wheels of their stars with exorbitant amounts of money.[1] You will need money to obtain quality equipment, slip unscathed through a scandal, protect your assets, or purchase helpful books like this one. Your fame is going to require a financial jumpstart to get going and a continual flow of funds for sustenance. We will further discuss the role of money in the next chapter, but from a capital standpoint, just remember now that a lack of money is a way to fail before you even get started.

PRODUCTION

As a business, you are offering a product, service, idea, or some combination of the three to the public, but in your enthusiasm to live in the spotlight, you can forget to ask one simple yet harsh preliminary question. Why? There are billions of other people, places, and things on which people can focus their attention. Why should they care about you or what you do? Now I'm not trying to hurt your feelings, but if you are business-minded, you need to think like a producer. And as a capitalistic producer, you cannot waste your time producing something that no one cares about. The answer to why, however, is very simple and the same for every successful business. **You produce because people want; you supply because there is a demand**.

Before you rip that runway, before you sing that verse, before you rehearse that line, you need to clearly define your potential fans and their desires. Then, you can cater to them. That is the recipe for success. Look for a hole and plug it. Look for a need and fill it.

Whatever you produce also needs to be something of quality. Take classes, go to school, practice, read books, get outside help, and do whatever you have to do to produce quality work. People today are increasingly able to tell when you are inferior. Also, consider cost effectiveness when producing. Sure, you may have to pay your dues at first, but if you continue to live in the red for extended periods, you should find ways to cut costs or boost revenue. Remember, your fame needs capital for you to continue to produce. As the saying goes, "If it doesn't make dollars, it doesn't make sense." If you're a hobbyist, then go ahead and produce for the sake of producing. However, if you want to be part of an industry, you will have to acknowledge customer needs. Create a quality product that effectively fills a void, and you will be starting off on the right foot.

EQUIPMENT

Quality equipment is another essential business element, and I define equipment not only as anything you use in your trade, but also anything you use to convey your fame. This could mean a flashy car, an eye-catching wardrobe, or supportive photos and videos. When it comes to equipment, I encourage you to always get the best that you can afford. Just like anything else, the equipment you use says so much about you, and the people you interact with will judge you on the equipment you have. I can't count the number of times I have been looked down upon for having an inexpensive keyboard. My $600 keyboard got the job done, but I fought an uphill battle at every audition before I played a single note. Every object that you surround yourself with reflects you and your taste, so before making your next purchase, consider its contribution to your fame.

UNDERSTANDING THE MARKET

When learning how to write my own business plan, I was surprised to see how much of it was related to other people and not me. I learned that I needed to include extensive research on the current state of the market, the competitors I would go up against, and the customers I would target. And in doing so, I began to understand that this is the diligent preparation that launches true stars and keeps them in the spotlight. You should be not only aware of yourself, but also have an understanding of everything around you. True fame is the result of months or even years of strategic planning. In order to make a splash, you have to know what is going to be hot years in advance and start working on it today. Sure, you can jump into the game with what has already been done, but there is a special place reserved for being the first, the new, the fresh, and the innovative.

Market research isn't as scary as it sounds. At the end of the day, it is simply finding answers to your most important questions. Who are your competitors? Do you want to take on Gisele Bundchen, or are you trying to be the star on your local runway? What does the public want now, and can you give it to them? What will the public want in the future? What are the trends, and where do things seem to be headed? Where are you headed in relation to the market? These are the kinds of questions that many of us fail to entertain as we focus only on ourselves and what we are trying to accomplish. Many people also skip the step of understanding the market because it takes a lot of time and effort to do this kind of research. Additionally, you can lack the humility to acknowledge that what you supply just simply may not be in demand. Several times, I have plowed through the first 30 pages of a business plan only to realize that my great idea wasn't so great at all. If you aren't aware of your surroundings, and if you don't read, research, and ask questions, you will charge ahead recklessly in an environment that is not conducive to your fame.

MARKETING

Marketing is one of my favorite business concepts and probably the most appealing task for a creative in the spotlight; however, those without a business background usually don't understand the extent of marketing. Marketing is not advertising. Advertising is a type of promotion, and promotion is only one of the four elements of marketing. Furthermore, marketing is not sales. The two are very connected, but they perform different functions. Using both strategically will set you apart when others think that they are one in the same. The common concept of proper marketing is based on four elements: product, price, distribution, and promotion. Marketing determines the presentation of the product, from how the packaging looks to how long the product will last. It involves setting a price that people will be willing to pay and determining what method you will use to physically move the product from your hand to the consumer's hand. And finally, promotion, the most commonly associated element of marketing, will determine how your product is communicated to the public. This usually involves some mix of personal selling, sales promotion, and advertising. These elements take a very interesting twist for someone in the spotlight, because as we discussed, you may be the product or personally intertwined with the product initially. As an integral part of the product or service, you will need to make decisions regarding your brand name, your "packaging," and more. You will have to price yourself, find ways to distribute yourself to many people, and communicate your offering through promotion. The whole process can seem surreal, but this is the mentality of industrialized fame and the gray area between personal and professional life.

Promotion will probably be the marketing element that you will focus on the most, particularly advertising which is a strategy implemented to reach large groups of consumers. Especially with the advancement and affordability of technology, the list of ways to advertise continues to expand. From television to internet, radio to billboards, flyers to direct mail, advertising is usually the go-to method of promotion for someone in the spotlight for many reasons. It is less time-consuming and less expensive than personal selling; it is conducive for marketing directly to consumers as opposed to middle men; and it works well for low-priced products and services. However, many who are striving for a life in the spotlight are not as familiar with personal selling or sales promotion, and depending on your situation and your goals, these methods may be effective for you as well.

Personal selling is a one-on-one promotional presentation, and it works well for high-priced items and business-to-business relations. For example, if you want to be a major recording artist, you need to promote to businesses that can take you further in addition to promoting to potential fans. Your approach to label executives, publicists, managers, and other key people will likely be in the form of a personal sell. Any advertising sent to them is sure to be thrown in the trash. Or, if you are auditioning for a movie role, you are essentially doing a personal sell for the casting director, so fine-tuning your personal sales approach will enhance your potential for upward mobility.

Sales promotions are also great career investments for stardom seekers that may increase sales down the road. We see sales promotions from marketers all the time, but I rarely see it implemented by those who want to be famous. This type of promotion is a one-time special event used to increase sales. It could be in the form of coupons, displays, samples, demonstrations, and more. If you are new, you must remember that people are skeptical of unknown products. They are less likely to spend their money on a questionable experience. The sales promotion fixes that problem by giving people an enticing taste of what you do. It is a necessary tool for establishing your brand, and when consumers are more familiar with your product, they will be more inclined to buy.

BRANDING

Strong branding is at the core of successful business. It is the conveyance of the identity and essence of a business in a clearly defined manner. In relation to fame, branding is a representation of who you are and what you are all about. It is a distinguishing design or name that separates you from the pack. Your fame, again, may require you to be heavily involved as the product. In this situation, you are essentially branding yourself, and this is easiest and most realistic when it is an extension of your individual uniqueness.

Also, as you continue to grow, you should focus on moving from personal integration with the product to personal integration with the brand. Being so involved in the product takes up a lot of your time and limits the extent of your reach. However, being more closely tied to the brand enables your product and other producers to produce exponentially for you, extending your fame without necessarily requiring your presence or constant attention. "The best way to stay famous is to find your way into multiple ventures in multiple media, and the best way to do that is to have an easily recognizable brand."[2] You should always try to find ways to bottle up your essence and mass produce it, whether it be through a duplicable product that lends itself to mass production (e.g. books, CDs, and radio/TV broadcasts) or some kind of franchising scenario in which others are trained to represent you (e.g. seminars, chain stores, and restaurants).

Developing a brand for your fame is easy when you observantly tap into your natural attributes. For example, I used to always wear a black Ventair cap. I would wear it to work. I would wear it to school. I would wear it to gigs. I would even wear it on dates. I don't know exactly why I liked it. I just did. I wore the hat so much that people began to associate it with my identity. This became apparent one day when I decided to try something different and wear a white hat. The uproar that resulted was very surprising to me, and I was inundated with questions: What happened? Why did you change? Does the white hat mean something different? It didn't take long for me to realize that people associated me with and recognized me by that hat.

Be aware of what people recognize about you and consider the things that you already latch onto. By wearing my Ventair hat all the time, I was sending a strong consistent message, whether I realized it or not. That wardrobe choice alone told people that I was dark and mysterious, faithful and dependable, and classy yet simple. The hat represented me so well that I eventually turned it into an essential part of my brand. I took promotional photos wearing the hat, and my logo became an Alfred Hitchcock-esque silhouette of me wearing the hat. "The stronger and more consistent your image, the more memorable as an individual you will become."[3] **Brand is about identity, and you will have less of a need to fabricate one when you discover the one you already have**.

Figure 9-1

In the spotlight, branding and iconography go hand in hand. Iconography freezes you in time and establishes a larger-than-life persona that coincides with the grand story of your fame. It is that one image or event that just stays in people's minds forever. Iconography is a whole other level of fame. Instead of being symbolized, as an icon, you become the symbol for something greater. It is an honor typically reserved for the best of the best…or the worst of the worst. For example, my Ventair cap logo was the symbol for me and my music, but Michael Jackson as the "King of Pop" was an icon for all pop music. Iconography can, however, have its downsides. To be forever remembered by a single moment in time can be damaging if that moment is negative. Even as you continue to grow and evolve, an iconic moment may keep your fans stuck in the past, hindering them from being receptive to new messages. American politician William Jennings Bryan remarked, "You cannot judge a man's life by the success of a moment…"[4] and those are good words to internalize for your personal development and self-esteem. But in fame, the general public will only know you through moments. So, you must make the most of your interactions, overwhelm the negative with positive, establish a quality brand, and be aware of iconographic situations.

SALES

Selling yourself can be a weird concept, but it is vital for fame. No one is going to put you on TV if you don't drive ratings. No one is going to give you a record deal if you don't have the potential to sell albums. No one is going to write about you if you don't move copies of the publication out the door. However, just as in the marketing process, when you sell yourself, you become the product and the producer. Again, this blurs the lines between your personage and enhances objectivism. Selling yourself puts an organism on the assembly line of an organization, and this process can feel very dehumanizing.

For instance, one drummer I worked with called himself a musical whore because he would play for any singer that offered him decent money, whether they were good or not. That thought stuck with me because I was doing the same thing to an even greater degree, never committing to a band that had no money, and proudly flaunting myself as a "hired gun." It's one thing to distribute a product to anyone, but quite another to distribute yourself to anyone, possibly compromising your valuable brand through the association. The supreme goal of business is profit, but a profit motive for a human product can easily turn you into a sort of prostitute who distributes services to the highest bidder. I wrestled with this concept for years, finally drawing a line in the sand and being more selective in my endeavors, even if it seemingly jeopardized my rise to fame. The idea of selling yourself may create an internal conflict for you as well, and rightfully so. The way you sell yourself may be a contentious personal decision that stems from your core, so consider your own situation. Will you place conditions on your sales, or will the highest bidder always win?

RELATIONSHIPS

If there was one thing that I really had to work hard on, it was networking. As I mentioned earlier, I am naturally quiet, so it was hard for me to figure out what to say to strangers. But even after discovering the important key of asking questions, I still found that I needed to have a better understanding of networking and an improvement on my ability to use it as an effective business tool. **Networking isn't just meeting people; it's meeting people with a purpose.** A good networker does his homework and understands his need for relationship. The person you are networking with has something you want from them. Define what that something is. You have something to offer them as well, and this too should be clearly defined. A good networker also treats the other person like an equal, not like a god or an object. If you slobber all over the person you are trying to network with, gushing praise, you may seem unprofessional. And, if you easily become star struck, that needs to stop now. You are a star too! Get on their level, and they will respect you. On the other hand, if it is obvious that you just want something from them, that may be a big turnoff as well. The entertainment industry is especially different from any other industry when it comes to networking. It thrives on networking like no other business, and **what you can do is absolutely secondary to who you know.** When evaluating your need for networking, think of fame as a swanky club; you can't get in unless you know somebody who knows somebody.

The Four Types Of Networking

I believe there are four kinds of effective networking: inward networking, outward networking, upward networking, and downward networking. You should network in all four ways and never neglect or belittle any one direction. You never know who you will meet, and each connection has the potential to advance you in several other directions. Our relationships can take a zigzag path in our lives, so networking creates valuable opportunities for exposure no matter where you are. Although it may seem daunting at first, if you are brave enough to put yourself out there and network with a genuine attitude, good things will come your way.

1. Inward Networking

Inward networking refers to securing and building airtight relationships with the people closest to you. An inner network is the balance you need when things on the outside are hectic. Networking in general takes guts because there is always the potential of getting burned, especially when networking out or up. **Your inner network, however, is like your nervous system. When it seems that you are reaching out to touch danger, it is the safety trigger that tells you to pull back**. For example, when I was mulling over the management agreement offered to me, I shared it with my inner network. I had such a desire for management that I wanted to sign the contract even though it didn't look all that great. However, the feedback from my inner network regarding that situation was negative, so I didn't sign. When my desire to network out said, "yes," my inner network said, "no," and protected me from a potentially bad situation. Find those special people who you can depend on for support and guidance, and include them in your inner network. Their strength and encouragement will give you the confidence needed to reach out in other directions.

2. Outward Networking

Networking out means getting to know as many people in as many connected fields as you can. It means identifying and reaching out to all the people who can benefit from what you offer and vice versa. For example, as a musician, I connect with anyone who uses live music: singers, rappers, producers, churches, schools, wedding planners, restaurants, corporations, and more. On the other hand, I also seek people that I need in order to produce music. That network includes musical equipment retailers, printers, designers, fellow musicians, rehearsal studios, publicists, and others. By consistently networking out, I can provide and obtain necessary resources. Although you should do as much as you can on your own, some things are best left to others. It is the power of networking out that exponentially increases the quality of your efforts. So, always look to be a help and receive help.

3. Upward Networking

Networking up is more focused on your specific career path. It is climbing the ladder, so to speak, and operating on a higher level that increases your fame. Networking out comparatively is the easy part, as unfortunately, opportunities to network up are usually very elusive. Sometimes it really is a matter of just being at the right place at the right time and being prepared when your number is called. In other cases, I have networked out to a person who has higher connections, which conveniently enabled me to network up through that person. There are so many doorways to networking up; however, you might not like what you see behind every door that you open. Hollywood, for instance, is notorious for having gatekeepers who will only let you network up through sexual acts, money, secret societies, and other suspect methods. You can really "sleep your way to the top" or "sell your soul to the devil" as they say. Those scenarios really do happen, so be prepared to respond to a sacrificial request. There is often a price to pay for networking up, as it is the most coveted form of networking, but just remain patient, diligent, and observant until your time comes. A step up can appear when you least expect it, and you have to be ready to shine at a moment's notice.

4. Downward Networking

When you are in the spotlight, you are placed on a pedestal. The people who place you on that pedestal are your fans, and you must not forget them. The most beloved celebrities make time for their fans. They visit kids in the hospital; they send handwritten letters; they sign autographs and take pictures. These kinds of relationships build a stronger bond than any kind of marketing campaign ever will. Networking down will also humble you, encourage you, and inspire you as you see how much of an impact you have on the lives of others and how deeply they want to support you. **As you show others love, they will show loyalty**.

EXIT STRATEGY

The brashness of my youth and my lack of real-world experience often led me to believe that things would always work, that plans would never fail, and that people would always like what I was doing. However, I could not escape the failure that even some of the most prominent people in the world have endured. The reality is that most people never reach the high level of fame they dream of. If you are smart enough and honest enough to realize when you have gone wrong, then you should also be resourceful enough to give yourself other options.

These days, I have endured so much failure that I have developed multiple backup plans should anything go wrong. And, looking back, I must say, I have survived in the spotlight this long because I have been a chameleon of sorts. I have always valued flexibility which allows me to easily fit into new situations or go in new directions. Sometimes you can be too stubborn by trying to make people accept what you have to offer. **But if you want to survive, you must be able to adapt**.

With an exit strategy, the pen is in your hand to write your own story. Take advantage of the control you have to choose your ending. If you are done with the spotlight, how will you leave? Will you retire slowly and gracefully, or will you crash and burn in the all-too-typical destructiveness of money, drugs, or sex problems? If you don't become a household name, then what will you do? Maybe you won't achieve a high level of fame. Maybe you won't be able to finance your dreams right now. Maybe you will become tired of the chase and give up on the spotlight all together. Regardless of your reasoning for ending up in another direction, if you don't have a plan, a world of depression, obscurity, loneliness, and hopelessness is waiting to eat you alive. Don't fall into that trap! **Failure at fame is not losing at life**. There are millions of other doors to walk through. Pick one and turn the handle. Just make sure you have an exit strategy before you enter!

■□■□■□■□■

The business items discussed here are just the tip of the iceberg, and although you do not have to be a business expert, you should know enough to enhance your fame and not become victimized. Business is a cycle of planning, executing, and evaluating. Thinking through this process will give you a broader perspective on the efforts required in the dark to sustain success in the spotlight. One of the most striking elements of the business perspective is that **before determining the people you need, you must understand the needs of the people**. The self-centered thought of "This is what I do; take it or leave it," will not fly in industrialized fame if what you do is not accepted. Humbling yourself enough to cater to your audience is the paradoxical method for further elevation.

Works Cited

1 (Borkowski 134,137)

2 (Montag and Pratt 100)

3 (Flocker 92)

4 (W. J. Bryan and M. B. Bryan)

THE ANSWER TO EVERYTHING IS...

UNDERSTANDING MONEY

Money is a large part of life in the spotlight. It just comes with the territory, but if you are not prepared to handle it, your unwise decisions can ruin you. Even if you don't think you have a lot of money now, you will still need to work on managing the amounts you do have. **More money will only expose your money management skills, not enhance them**. If you are struggling to manage $30,000 a year, what makes you think you can handle $3,000,000? Moreover, before you think about handling the big bucks, you should seek to increase your knowledge about money, especially as it relates to the business of your fame. And, the first step to dealing with money as with just about anything else is understanding exactly what it is.

Money Is Worthless; It's Perception Is Valuable

Money is worthless pieces of paper made from trees and little hunks of metal made from rocks. That's it. Money is rocks and trees. We use it for commerce, or even more simply, for trading. Yet, it only has value because we give it value. It is a quantifiable measurement that translates our work into purchasing power and allows us to buy goods and services. If you boil money down to these core definitions, you will have a better perspective on it and know how to maximize your use of it. Our money used to be backed by gold, but now it is the perceived value that gives it such enormous power. In fact, it's common for people to aggressively pursue it to the point of killing others to obtain it. Intrinsically, money is worthless, but its purchasing power can literally change our lives. With money, you can buy just about anything, including much of the resources needed to become famous. It puts you on the fast track to fame by instantly giving you access.

Money Is Shaky Ground

Money is very similar to fame in its instability. It can increase or decrease in value, be earned over time, or be lost in an instant. It can be misplaced, found, or won. It can be given to you or stolen from you. It can be plentiful, or it can be scarce. But no matter your circumstance, you never seem to have enough money. Just like fame, when you get to the place where you have enough money, another plateau appears, and "enough" is no longer satisfying. The concept of inflation alone means that your dollar is worth less with each passing day, forcing you to increase your cash flow for survival.

As you saw in the toss theory, money and fame are not good foundations on which to base your life because of this instability. Your worth is not dependent on monetary amounts, and you should always see yourself as a valuable person regardless of the money you have. Remember, money is rocks and trees. You are not your money, and your intrinsic value and contentment should not be based on it. However, your financial situation usually becomes depressing when you compare yourself to others. The infamous goal of "keeping up with the Joneses" is what creates a continual dissatisfaction. And if you are famous and the Joneses are millionaires, keeping up can become much more difficult. In these kinds of situations, you can easily be unaware of how rich you actually are. We are so shielded in America, considering a $34,000-a-year job to be average, when in fact that salary puts you in the top 11% of the richest people in the world![1] You may have heard these types of global financial statistics before, but have they really sunk in? Even if you have the money to purchase this book, you are richer than most.

It is usually easy to tell which people allow their lives to revolve around money. When they have it, they feel superior to others, and when they don't, they feel like a nobody. Both are bad situations for anyone in the spotlight. A feeling of superiority results in an arrogance that will alienate your fans and compromise your fame, while a lack of confidence will also be unappealing and destructive to your fame. The answer, like always, falls in the middle.

When it comes to money, you should strive to find contentment in your current financial situation, yet be confident in your ability to excel and make more money. Contentment, however, is not comfort. Comfort makes you fat and lazy. You should always want to have a drive for more money because it is an important tool for increasing your fame and expanding your influence. **Contentment will allow you to enjoy your fame, but comfort will kill it**. If your ultimate goal is money, then you are reading the wrong book. I'm sorry that you have made it this far, but there are much easier ways of making money than trying to be famous. Riches and comfort may be a kindred cause and effect scenario, but fame and comfort are opposing ideals.

Money Is A Private Mirror

There is an interesting Bible verse in Matthew 6:21 that states, "For where your treasure is, there your heart will be also,"[2] and I have found this to be so true in my life and in the lives of others. The way in which someone uses money can be very telling. Money is important in fame, and when you exchange it for something else (a dinner, the lotto, education, an event, an experience, etc.) you show that what you obtain is important to you as well. For example, thousands of dollars have been invested in this book, indicating that it was important for me to get this information published. Similarly, you have used your money to purchase a copy of this book. That shows that being famous is important to you.

The money-importance correlation, however, can be used to spot inconsistencies as well. When your money usage does not reflect your goals, it can signify internal confusion or conflict. If your goal is to be famous, but all your money goes towards just looking famous, you are sabotaging your said goal with your actions and placing more importance on appearance than achievement. As another example, if your money goes to drugs before essentials like food and clothing, that indicates a serious disruption in your life balance as drugs have taken an erroneous foundational position. Your money is a mirror that reflects you and your values. Take a look at it often and evaluate the integrity with which you pursue your goals. In addition to knowing where your money goes, you should also know why it goes there.

Money Is A Public Monitor

The ability of your fame to generate financial reward is a significant mile marker for the level of your fame. When people use their purchasing power to buy what you are producing, despite the many other ways in which they can spend their money, it is an indication of your value and your connection to others. Although it can be difficult to measure fame, it is very easy to measure money. So, analyzing the income generated by your fame in the following areas will help you quantify your success to some degree.

> **The demand for you fame:** How often is your product or service requested?

> **The value of your fame:** How much are people paying for your products or services?

> **The extent of your fame:** Where are people purchasing your products or services?

The impact of your fame: Are people coming back to purchase more, or is one time enough?

Providing answers to these types of questions will be helpful, but remember that this is just a general indicator. Fame and money may not always directly correlate. You may be known, but that might not always translate to a great amount of monetary compensation. On the other hand, you may be relatively unknown and still receive money from all over.

Money Requires Priority Decisions

Money and fame are like two brothers. Sometimes they play nice, but at other times, they just don't get along so well. For example, you could be offered a high-paying job that leads to obscurity while being offered an opportunity which pays nothing but offers an increase in fame. Which will you choose? Or perhaps you may have an opportunity to increase your money, but as a result you are likely to lose many of your fans. Will you take that opportunity? These are personal decisions that come up early and often in your career, sometimes before you even get started. We usually think of fame and fortune together, but at times you will have to prioritize one over the other. Some decisions may be handled on a case-by-case basis, while others may require you to rest on your laurels.

Money Is A Symbol Of Affluence

Like several other factors in life, money tends to separate people into one of three categories: a small upper class, a small lower class, and a large middle class. Our society is structured in such a way that only a few reach that upper level, and those who reach it lead a completely different life in nearly every way. They even receive a broad range of reactions to their status from the other classes, ranging from resentment and jealousy to fear and intimidation to idolization and inspiration. Sound familiar? The same can be said about the life of a famous person, and the plateau you reach at a high level with either money or fame are strikingly related. **Therefore, it's worthwhile to consider climbing the ladder of monetary success and crossing over to fame or, better yet, attaining monetary success that coincides step-by-step with your fame**. Breaking through into the spotlight and increasing status are difficult, so these monetarily stimulated approaches may be easier ways for you to move forward to fame. If money takes care of your elevation, then you are already operating on a high level. At that point, your only other need will be exposure.

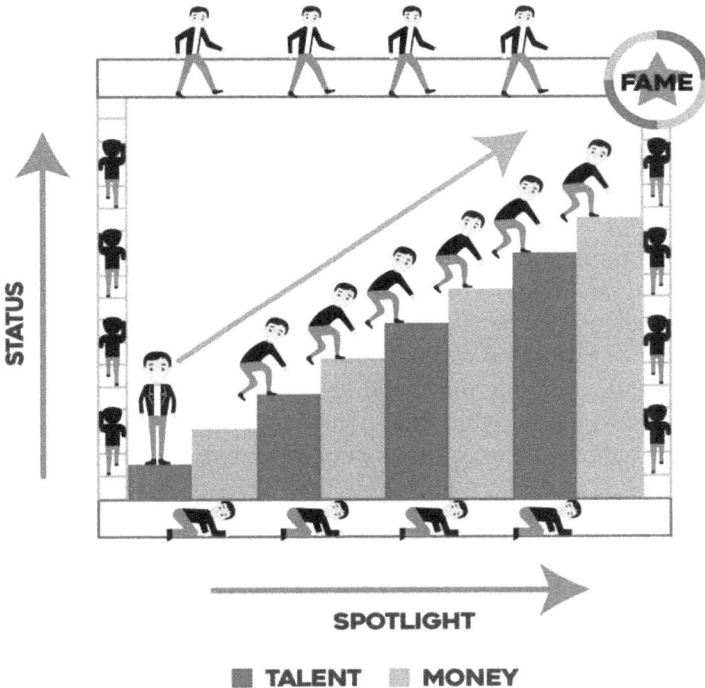

Figure 10-1

Money Is A Tool Of Influence

So often, we think of the good that money can bring us, but it works in reverse as well, taking away the bad. Put simply, money can make many things, people, and problems seemingly disappear. Remember, a life of celebrity is not all fun and games, and a person in the spotlight will always have more issues than the average person. Usually in the form of a secret or legal issue, these career-threatening situations can be sidestepped by throwing a little cash at the instigator. It sounds manipulative, but you have to fight fire with fire. With all of the instances in which fame and fortune conflict, you should take advantage of the times when they can complement each other. If your fame is in jeopardy, fight with your money. If your money is in jeopardy, fight with your fame.

MAKING MONEY

Your ability to be yourself should not hinge on the amount of money you have; however, your ability to be famous and the scope of your influence absolutely depends on money. **In a capitalistic society, fame is valued because it makes money**. You must capitalize on fame; otherwise, it will be worthless to others. **A life in the spotlight is an extraordinary life with extraordinary needs; therefore, it requires extraordinary dollars**. As I mentioned in the previous chapter, your fame is actually a business. Businesses require work, work requires people, and people require compensation for their work—the most motivating compensation being money. You can't get around it. If you plan on being famous, there has to be a financial component somewhere.

Your fame and its perpetuation require money, whether it's your money or someone else's. You may not see the money. You may not receive the money. But, somewhere along the line, there is a paper trail making you famous. Even for those on reality shows who seem like average people, millions of dollars have gone into producing those shows so that we can see those people. No matter what their personal paycheck is, the dissemination of their fame requires large amounts of corporate dollars. Now for stars who command higher fees, you might think they have more than enough money to be famous. Yet, we still constantly hear of celebrity financial woes. The million-dollar Hollywood deal may sound like more than enough, but how much of that money goes into the stars' pockets? As you will see in the example below, the expenses that may be required for a life of fame can add up quickly, leaving you with a lot less than what you started with.

Let's pretend you are an actor who just received his first big break. You are filming a movie that is going to give you a gross income of $1,000,000 this year. But first things first, Uncle Sam is going to want his share immediately. With the amount of money you are making, you will owe around 35% in taxes. A business manager is usually necessary to handle these large sums, and perhaps your investments and other transactions. So, just add another 5% or $50,000 to that bill. Now, with a number of write-offs, you can actually pay a smaller percentage in taxes. But for this example, let's just say right off the bat that you're down to 40%.

$600,000 is still a lot of money, but you don't just walk into this kind of fortune. You have to be connected, or more commonly, know someone who is connected. That someone is your agent. He's going to want 10% off the top as well. Now, you're down to $500,000. However, since you are working full time on a movie, you have no time to run the business of your fame. A 12 to 15-hour day is common in the film industry, and now you don't have time to run anything else in your life either. You're going to need a personal manager for the reasonable price of 15%. Now, you're down to $350,000.

Since you are also a heart throb, screaming fans stalk you, the paparazzi flocks wherever you go, and jealous lovers send you hate mail. You don't feel so safe anymore, so you hire a bodyguard. A decent one for daily security will run you about $150,000. You now have $200,000 left, which is just enough for the down payment on your new million-dollar house. It's a necessity. You're a celebrity now, and you can't be seen in your crummy, old apartment. So, congratulations! You are now completely broke. And by the way, you haven't bought any food, you are still driving your old car, you are still wearing your old clothes, you haven't made any mortgage or property tax payments, you haven't obtained a publicist, and your lawyer also has a hefty legal bill waiting for you.

Hopefully you receive the profits of your fame, but as you saw in the previous example, many other people can profit before you do. Your fame will need to grow for you to continue to be famous, and growth in business means continually increasing profit. Remember, growth is life, and if you are not growing, you are dying. **If what you are doing doesn't make a suitable profit, you will either go nowhere or possibly give up on your fame altogether**. Spotlight seekers often obtain a traditional job to finance their fame in the beginning, and the most iconic example is probably the actor who waits tables to get by. A supporting job can be an excellent jumpstart for your fame; however, this double life is problematic if your fame does not support itself eventually. At this juncture, many fall off the path to fame because their side venture becomes more and more prominent and permanent. You can easily lose focus as other life events like marriage, children, or health issues begin to take over. At this point, you fall into a cycle of constantly infusing capital into an unprofitable endeavor. **Prioritize the goal of self-sufficient fame, and count the costs before you cash the checks. Making money puts dollars on the table, but making profit puts dollars in your pocket**.

If you are receiving a different trade that you deem equally as valuable as financial profit, such a trade could be beneficial for you in the short term. An internship, for example, may give you valuable experience that can be used for future profitability. However, in some areas, the internship concept is commonly abused, and certain people and organizations will not hesitate to exploit your work without much of a fair trade. I did an unpaid radio promotion internship for a small record label, and on my last day, they said that they may have a job for me. But after that, I never heard from them again. They obtained a lot of work from me, but I received very little experience and no future profitability from them. That is the kind of situation you should avoid, and ideally, you should seek opportunities to both learn and receive payment. For example, if you are new to acting, I recommend that you become an extra for a while just to get your feet wet. Doing this will give you the chance to learn what it is like to be on set and network with other actors and crew while still receiving a few dollars for your work. Increasing income and information simultaneously is the most efficient use of your time.

Your ability to make money is much more valuable than the money you make, and your efforts to protect yourself should be greater than your efforts to protect your money. Personal development pioneer Shakti Gawain explains, "The more we learn to operate in the world based on trust in our intuition, the stronger our channel will be and the more money we will have."[3] Neglect of your physical, mental, social, emotional, and spiritual components may inhibit your ability to make money. Too often we think of our job as the goose that lays the golden eggs. However, the most powerful wealth-generating factor lies within us, not our jobs. You are the goose that lays the golden eggs! Sure, you should take care of the eggs, but if you lose the eggs, you can make more. If you lose your job, you can obtain another one. If you lose your money, you can make more. You, however, are irreplaceable. Value the goose over the eggs. The eggs come and go, but you're in trouble once the goose is cooked!

If you're unable to make money at any period of time, you should not let that completely stop your activities. You can create without money. Don't wait until you have enough money to do something that you feel called to do. Doing nothing is the same as going backwards, and if you wait for money, you may be waiting forever. **Never let a dollar put the brakes on your career**. Oliver Wendell Holmes sadly noted, "Most of us go to our graves with our best music still inside us, unplayed."[4] Do what you can right now! Do something for your fame today, despite your current economic circumstance. This will teach you to use creativity. Learn how to operate outside of money when you lack it. Don't worry at first if what you are doing looks cheap or bad. A great voice on a cheap recording will still get someone's attention. Just ask Justin Bieber, Jay Pharoah, and Korean pop star Psy. They all skyrocketed into fame by simply posting inexpensive videos on YouTube. **Everything you do, even if it is a failure, is a stepping stone to success**. Don't be overly concerned with how the money will come. If you keep working despite financial struggles, things just tend to work out in the end, even if it is not in the manner you expected. Learn from your mistakes and adjust your plan, but keep planning and creating your fame. Don't wait for the spotlight to appear. Be bold enough to step onto the dark stage. Once you do, the lights will come on.

MANAGING MONEY

The money that you make is useless if you don't know how to handle it. If you have poor money management now, your ineptitude will stay with you and probably get worse as you increase in fame. Still, for some reason, we tend to have this idealistic conception that if we had much more money, then all of our management problems would be solved. But in reality, as Biggie Smalls said, the opposite is what usually occurs: "Mo money, mo problems."[5] The little mistakes you make with your money today will become catastrophes in the spotlight. Money management issues have wreaked havoc in the lives of many celebrities. If you don't like dealing with or managing money, then now is the time for you to change if you want to maximize your fame and control your own destiny. Passing your financial obligations off to someone else when you don't have a clue is a recipe for disaster. You don't have to become a CPA, but understanding some basic ideas of money management will help you in the long run.

The list of stars who have had disastrous money problems is quite long. Toni Braxton, Billy Joel, Gary Busey, Lindsay Lohan, Michael Vick, Natalie Cole, Scott Storch, Mike Tyson, MC Hammer, Kim Basinger, Donald Trump, and Burt Reynolds are just a few of the many celebrities who have filed for bankruptcy at some point in their lives.[6] A horde of other stars have also had significant money issues. Former NFL running back Travis Henry reportedly fathered 11 children with 10 different women, and now pays an estimated $170,000 annually in child support.[7] According to *Business Insider*, Wesley Snipes received a 3-year prison sentence for failing to pay 17 million in taxes.[8] And even Michael Jackson died with 323 million in debt.[9] Head the warning signs. Money management is a big issue, and these celebrity troubles are not just a coincidence.

Good money management is all about perspective. It requires you to think about the past, present, and future. Just ask yourself three simple questions: What past debts do you owe? What are your current wants and needs? How can you best set yourself up for the future? Good money management addresses past money, present money, and future money effectively in a manner that allows each area to get attention. Problems occur when too much monetary emphasis is placed in a single time frame. If you have exorbitant amounts of debt, it will inhibit your ability to operate in the present and future. If you spend all your money now, you will not reap the leveraging benefits of borrowing, nor will you have anything for the future should your circumstance change. And lastly, if you stock pile for the future, again you will miss out on the power of borrowing, and your present will be limited and less enjoyable. The magic word again is…say it with me…balance. It can be difficult, but if you learn to balance your money in the past, present, and future, you will be on the right track in regards to money management.

Obtaining balanced money management can be easier said than done, and although I have improved, I still struggle with it today. In my own experience, I would manage the present well. I was not a big spender, and I would never mind a slightly uncomfortable present. Growing up, my present was always uncomfortable, so I had a natural desire to manage present money well as an adult. However, I would never have a balanced past or future. I let bills and debts pile up and accumulate interest. I had charge-offs, and I ruined my credit. I never saved for emergencies, and whenever calamity struck, I was out on a limb asking for financial help from others. I had no significant investments or assets. I always worked for money; my money never worked for me. If I had great fame at that time, it would have been disastrous, but luckily my financial fires were small enough to put out in a few years. Now, I currently have no unmanageable debts, I live modestly yet more comfortably in the present, and I have created investments that will enhance my future.

The concept of managing money is really a matter of developing a plan, and that plan is called a budget. Whether you have 10 dollars or 10 million dollars, you should get in the habit of budgeting now. Operating without a budget is like putting together a complicated machine with no instructions, and if you do not budget, you are more likely to fail financially. Successful budgeting for growth requires you to widen the gap between income and expenses for maximum profitability. This is accomplished by always seeking opportunities to increase your income while lowering your expenses. However in your planning, estimate high expenses and a more conservative income. This will create breathing room for unexpected events and enable your predictions to be a bit more accurate. Budgeting will also give you a picture of yourself over time, and with a good budget in place, you should be able to more clearly identify your financial strengths and weaknesses.

The placement of your money is also a significant part of management. Don't tell anyone how much money you make if they don't need to know. Don't let anyone handle your money for you if you don't know anything about them, or if you don't have at least a basic understanding of what they are doing. And, try not to keep a large amount of money on you or in your house. Keeping a stash under your mattress might work for $20, but if you have $20,000, you might want to find a safer place. Learn as much as you can on your own, but also seek the advice of trusted financial advisors. The higher you go, the more you will need to discuss items like living wills and trusts, multiple accounts, incorporation, the creation of charities and foundations, and more. If you just drop your first million into your checking account and call it a day, you will have already begun to squander your funds.

You have worked hard for that million, so now make that million work hard for you.

Lastly, we have already seen that fame makes you a target, but money also obviously increases your risk of being targeted. Gangs and thieves or even friends and family may all have an eye on your money. In fact, you can even be targeted by the government as they love to make examples out of people, the most visible example being a celebrity. Sometimes celebrities aren't behaving as badly as we think they are. They are just regular people under a more watchful eye, destined to be criticized for any misstep. For instance, how many times have you seen high profile individuals busted for tax evasion? It happens pretty often and becomes a big news story that strongly *encourages* the rest of us to pay our taxes. There are several entities constantly watching the high earners, and those who do not diligently manage their money always run the risk of being targeted.

On the other hand, I have met many millionaires, and there are two commonalities that I have noticed that protect them from targeting. First, they rarely look or act like millionaires in the stereotypical sense. Most of the richest people I have met look pretty average. They drive middle-class cars and wear thrifty clothes. They are not gaudy and they normally do not attract attention to themselves unless their fame requires it. Secondly, they can account for every cent they have. It takes even more of an economical mentality to accumulate that much money, and an awareness to hold onto it. Being able to account for your money means that you know what is going on and that you are in control. Knowing that they are prey, those millionaires wisely camouflage to fool predators. It would behoove us all to do the same.

SPENDING MONEY

When we obtain large amounts of money, the natural urge is to spend it. In fact, that is what most of us do. In a survey of 3,000 Americans conducted by Rasmussen Reports, half of the participants spent more than they earned.[10] As we have seen in the news headlines, celebrities are subject to the same financial desires, and spending issues don't automatically go away with fame or fortune. Whether you are famous or not, rich or poor, you can get into serious trouble when your spending desires overshadow your other financial obligations.

Spending money is the present management of money that usually connects us with pleasure and comfort. Although some of the aforementioned celebrities may have just had some bad luck, several have been obviously overindulgent. Paying a past debt or waiting for a future payoff is unappealing, while present spending preys on our hedonistic tendencies. And, with a big jump in our discretionary income, it can be easy to go wild as we seek happiness and fulfillment. Now, I'm not going to tell you that you shouldn't spend money and that money doesn't buy happiness, because well, I would be lying. Our economy doesn't flow unless people spend, and according to the New York Times article, *Don't Indulge, Be Happy*, "people with a comfortable living standard are happier than people living in poverty."[11] So, spending money is a perfectly fine mood-elevating experience, but if you constantly find yourself in financial jams, you may need to curb your spending so that you have more of a financial cushion.

5 Ways To Regulate Spending

Take a look at the following ideas for spending control, and determine how you can incorporate each into your famous living financial management plan.

1. Be Realistic

While it is important to control spending, if you are going to be in the spotlight, there will be intense pressure to simultaneously look the part. **Fame by definition requires you to be outstanding, and you can't be outstanding and average at the same time**. This is the battle you fight between the conservative thinking of your normal life and the liberal extravagance that may be associated with your life in the spotlight. It's important to draw a line in the sand between fantasy and reality. And with that in mind, let's get one thing straight: Television is not real! I'm sorry to burst your bubble, but even reality shows are scripted. The flashy music videos you see on television are not reality. They are fantasy, so don't overextend yourself financially to live that way. I have been in television shows, movies, commercials, and music videos. And, it is all fake. The girls are hired workers. The cars are rented. The bling is borrowed. There are body doubles, stunt doubles, pounds of makeup, wigs, and age-reversing lighting, all to create an illusion. Don't try to turn your reality into that fantasy. This will lead to wasteful spending and distorted fame priorities.

2. Take Control

If you buy everything your beady little eyes see, that is a sign that you are not in control of yourself. You have slipped from indulgence to overindulgence. You are clay in the advertiser's hands. You may be propelled by internal greed, or you may be jealous of your neighbor. At any rate, you continue to buy, even if your purchases are unnecessary. When you spend in this manner, you do not control your possessions; your possessions control you. However, you can take control back by understanding the motivations behind your purchases and being selective about which motivations you act on. Ask yourself, "What is the purpose of my possession?" A natural disaster scenario is one trick that I use to evaluate the necessity of a possession in my life. I imagine what objects I would try to salvage if something happened to my house. This exercise will really help you separate needs and wants. Knowing the difference between the two, and denying yourself of your more frivolous wants will help you in the long run, not only financially but in other areas of your life as well.

3. Change The Range

Another great way to approach your spending is to change the range. By that, I mean changing the range of money available for you to spend and living on less than what you make. You can accomplish this by either spending less or making more. For example, instead of using a range of 100% of my money, I try to limit my spending to 70% of what I make. Then, I use the rest for gifts, savings, and investments. If I can't afford something within my 70% limit, I consider it unaffordable for me, and I don't buy it. Also, I only borrow money for emergency situations or necessities, never for pleasure. Since adopting these rules, I have never had any substantial money problems. Nevertheless, this can be hard to do, even for the most frugal. I too lost just about everything I had before adopting this rule. But, often such a crisis is necessary to cause us to change.

This idea of living below your means only works though if you make enough to be satisfied or at least survive. I could never live on 70% if I made minimum wage. On the other hand, if I made more money than I do now, I could more easily live on the 70% or possibly less. The range of values you have to work with changes the dollar amount of the percentage, so in essence, you maintain your current spending level without overextending yourself if you just make more. Adopting these rules also meant that I had to turn down jobs. That was difficult to do, because I was used to accepting everything that came along. But, with these percentages, I figured out that at a certain dollar amount per hour, I would not be able to function financially the way I would like to. I had to develop the patience and the higher self-worth perspective to turn down certain jobs in order to be available for the ones that paid the wage I needed.

4. Just Wait

Like a true advertiser, Nike says, "Just Do It," but I say, "Just Wait!" You will be surprised at how much your feelings change regarding a purchase over time. You may not be able to live without that new car one day, then not care at all about it a week later. So, you can test out your true feelings about a purchase by simply waiting. If you still want the object of your desire a day, a week, a month, or even a year later, then you know that the desire is genuine.

Now obviously, this is usually for large purchases. You shouldn't wait a year for a candy bar! Allow some impulsivity for small objects. But, for significant purchases like a big screen TV or a top-of-the-line musical instrument, consider waiting a few weeks or a few months just to see if you still feel the same way. If you choose to adopt this method, it will require a great deal of patience on your part as many advertisers play on your weakness to consume impulsively. However, if you wait, you may find something else that is better. Many times, I have changed my mind altogether and was glad I didn't waste my money on a purchase that I didn't really want.

5. Become a Druggie

In light of the previous chapters, I know the heading of this section may be startling, but just hear me out. There is only one drug that I will endorse, and that is OPM (pronounced opium). I'm not talking about the narcotic drug. OPM stands for other people's money, and a great way to stop spending so much of your own money is to start spending someone else's! That may sound negative to you, but OPM is a positive and common practice. When you incur a debt, you are using someone else's money to get what you need right now. When you accept charitable contributions, you are using other people's money as well. Small businesses are started with capital investments, corporations are run off the money of stockholders, churches collect tithes and offerings, and the list goes on and on. Open your mind and think in other methods of exchange before you spend all your dollars. Ask yourself, "How can I initiate a transaction that does not require me to spend my own money?" The easy way out is to throw your own money at a situation, but if fame is also your goal, OPM should be a top priority for you. This method will not only relieve financial pressure to spend, but it will also create the networking that will allow your fame to spread in new directions.

Additionally, when you view money as a means of trading, you will understand when you don't have to use it. You can trade with other things besides money. We get so caught up in spending dollars that we don't consider the other means of exchange. **Remember, money is a tool, but there are many other tools available. You may love to write with a pencil, but there are pens, markers, crayons, and chalk available to you.** People will trade goods and services for recognition, food, swag, souvenirs, experience, opportunity, and more. Even your fame can be currency.

SAVING MONEY

Saving is similar to investing in that it works on borrowing and lending and is a sacrifice of present comfort. It is an interesting concept that we are usually taught at an early age; however, you were probably not taught that your piggy bank will always have a hole in it called inflation. Inflation gives you a picture of your purchasing power by measuring the change in prices over time. Simply put, the higher the inflation rate, the less you can buy with the money you have saved. Inflation is also important to consider when dealing with interest, or the cost of borrowing.

Depending on interest rates and inflation rates, you can lose, break even, or increase your money when putting it away. For instance, I knew a guy who hated banks. He would keep all his money with him because he thought that banks would steal from him. However, by keeping his money, it actually became worth less and less. If the inflation rate was 3% that year, his purchasing power would drop 3% that year as well. It doesn't sound like much, but doing this for 20 or 30 years will always send you backwards. This also depends on how much money you are working with. Three percent on a million dollars is a big loss! His alternative would be to open a savings account with a bank. When you have a savings account, you are essentially letting the bank borrow your money. In return, they pay you an interest rate for lending to them. But, unfortunately savings rates for banks are typically lower than inflation. For example, your savings account may pay 1% interest, while the inflation rate is 3%. In this scenario, your money would actually be worth 2% less over time. So, even in a savings account, you are still losing money! You're just not losing as much money as you would be if you acted as my friend did and stuffed your cash in a sock drawer.

Savings accounts, however, are not all negative, and I still recommend them at least in the short term because the pros can outweigh the cons. Savings accounts allow for liquidity, meaning that you can easily access your cash whenever you need it. If you are in a fix, and you need cash quickly, it is great to have a savings account. Usually minimum balances start at one dollar, so the barrier to entry is extremely low. And lastly, a savings account with a bank means safety, especially when the bank is FDIC insured. That federal insurance will cover you up to $100,000 should anything happen to your money while it is in the bank. If you are robbed, and thieves find a stash in your mattress, you may be just out of luck.

I qualified the benefits of a savings with a short-term range (less than a year) because I believe that is the extent of their usefulness unless you are creating an emergency fund. I would be willing to sacrifice the purchasing power in order to have the liquidity and safety. On the other hand, if I am saving for a purchase, it will typically be something I can buy within a year. I believe that with the inflation and interest rate differences, any kind of long term savings is inefficient. For anything long term, you will want your interest rate to exceed inflation.

INVESTING MONEY

Money is a tool, but the ultimate use of that tool is through investing. **Even though most Americans invest in some way, if money was a hammer, you would find that many people still like to collect hammers instead of building houses**. Investing is exponential growth, and exponential growth should draw the attention of anyone seeking fame. But often, we can be fooling ourselves when it comes to investments that are truly assets.

I love Robert Kiyosaki's approach of investing in real assets, not hidden liabilities. He simply defines assets as anything that produces more for you and liabilities as anything that takes money from you.[12] With that definition, he denounces the asset classification of personal houses, cars, some businesses, and other desires we typically associate with riches. To him, they are liabilities which pose as assets. These liabilities take your valuable time or money for upkeep when you could be making more money elsewhere. Instead, he recommends that your asset list include investments like stocks, bonds, mutual funds, royalties, businesses that don't require your presence, income-generating real estate and other similar ventures. The goal is to have as much of your income generated from your investments and less of it generated from your job. The more you can reap from your investments, the more you can focus on the business of your fame. And, if you really want to go for the gold, pursue avenues such as businesses, products, buildings, and intellectual properties where you can attach your brand, increasing your fame and your money simultaneously.

I also view giving as an investment. When you send money out, there is always a return. Giving operates on a universal law of seed and harvest. Whenever you plant a seed, you reap a harvest exponentially greater than the seed that you planted. This applies in every facet of life. If you give hate, people will tend to hate you back. If you give help, the people you help will want to return the favor. Whenever you give, you are bound to receive. It might be something different than what you gave, but you will definitely get something back in return. You should give expecting to receive. There is always an exponential increase when it comes to giving, so I really consider it an investment. Giving money also perpetuates your fame because it builds relationship on a deeper level. It is a way to influence, reaching the highest part of the tree of stable stardom. It is an automatic positive encounter with you that multiplies your fame.

When actor Bill Murray was asked about being rich and famous, he sarcastically remarked, "...try being rich first...when you become famous, you end up with a 24-hour job."[13] Always the entertainer, Murray's comment was comical; however, it was also very profound. Becoming rich is difficult, but comparatively, the statistics show that being famous on a high level is a nearly impossible feat reserved for a select few. Despite your talents, your connections, and your work ethic, the potential for fame is still dismal. For example, investing in fame is one of the most unwise investments anyone can make from a strictly financial perspective. I would never invest in a music group…and I'm a musician! Still, our sense of identity can be so strongly connected to fame that we continue our pursuits, despite the odds. Murray's comment is striking, and hopefully you are beginning to see the powerful lesson in his words that I have expounded upon in this chapter. **Put simply, if money is a link to not only obtaining but also maintaining fame, and of the two, money is easier to obtain, then make money first**. The best way to do this is with capital investments from outside supporters or through income-generating investments like real estate, businesses, royalties, stocks, bonds, and mutual funds, not with a crummy job that takes you away from the spotlight, kills your spirit, and slows your growth. Your investments don't even have to be related to your fame as long as they provide stable capital generation that you can use for fame endeavors until your fame is self-sufficient.

Additionally, a money-first approach can benefit you in several growth-oriented ways. It will enable you to develop essential business skills, do some trial and error with the perils and protections of fame without the media tracking your every success and failure, increase your networking opportunities, relieve some of the pressure of profitability, combat the struggling artist mentality, and position you for crossover and branding, all while providing a stable financial foundation that also functions as a built-in exit strategy. If you prioritize wealth generation, your fame then becomes a quirky investment and not the crux of your entire life.

■□■□■□■□■□

Money is a very interesting tool that reveals the deep characteristics of its users. And, depending on your management abilities, it can propel you to the top or bring you down to destruction. Money truly is the key to the exponential increase that enables you to be famous at the highest levels, and although you may need an infusion of cash from an outside source to get you started, your fame needs to eventually carry its own weight and generate income. If it doesn't, you will have a draining hobby that stagnates you, not a profitable business that elevates you. Your fame must make money or show money-making potential, or it will just not grow. And without financial growth, you will hit the wall that most people hit and eventually fail at stardom. So, with an eye on the past, present, and future, strive to create a financial plan that uses borrowing, spending, saving, and investing as strategic leverages that will make your journey much smoother. Remember, fame is unstable, but with a little bit of financial security, you will be more prepared to handle the possibilities.

Works Cited

1 (Winograd)

2 (*NIV*, Matt. 6:21)

3 (Gawain 192)

4 (Holmes 99)

5 (The Notorious B.I.G.)

6 (Williams)

7 (Martinez et al.)

8 (Kelley)

9 ("Michael Jackson")

10 (Kavoussi)

11 (Dunn and Norton)

12 (Kiyosaki and Lechter 12)

13 (Macnab)

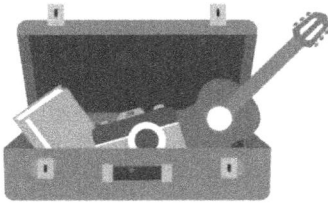

11
PREPARING
FOR THE
POSSIBILITIES

The fairytale of fame always exists in the reality of life, and we should never forget that. No matter how much we desire fame, we cannot guarantee it. The most we can do is structure our lives in such a way that fame becomes more likely and prepare for the possibilities. This book has covered many ways by which you can prepare your life for fame, and if it seems overwhelming, then you have truly grasped the concept. The overwhelming number of details within this life construct however, can be summed up in four major steps that will position you for sustainable fame.

First, you must fix your infrastructure. Anything without a solid foundation is sure to fall. You must obtain strength and stability in as many life areas as possible so that you will be able to stand when things get tough…and they will get tough.

Next, you must arrange a course of action. Remember, fame doesn't just happen. You create it, you shape it, you build it. You have to determine what success means for you, create goals, and develop a plan that gets you there or at least places you in opportunistic situations.

When developing your course of action, however, you need to remain open and flexible to different paths because there will be opposition. A couple of doors may swing wide open, but a thousand will slam in your face. So, this third step of mastering the difficulties will require you to endure a process of growth. Fame is not easy to achieve, and it's even more difficult to sustain. Why? Because the obstacles are big enough to stop most people. So, there is no reason to be shocked when you get hit by the hindrances. You must become a master of changing *can't* into *can*, *no* into *yes*. When you are weak, the difficulty will always be bigger than you, but when you have grown, you will become the bigger entity and have the perspective to see a way to make things work.

Lastly, if you really want long-lasting fame, you need to always seek to establish a deep connection. Don't worry if you can't do this with everyone; you're not supposed to. If you did, it would counter one of the purposes of the deep connection, which is the exponential growth of your fame. If you do something cool in front of 10 people, they might post it on Twitter, talk about it on Facebook, or maybe tell a friend or two. On the other hand, if you change the lives of 10 people, they will eagerly send others to you and become life-changers themselves in a way that honors you. **With a surface connection, you create moments, but with a deep connection, you create momentum**. The deep connections seem more difficult, but they will actually lighten your load because you won't have to pick up followers one at a time.

So, once you **F**ix the infrastructure, **A**rrange the course of action, **M**aster the difficulties, and **E**stablish the deep connection, you have created the outline for your **FAME**! At this point, you leave the rest in God's hands and let time and chance play their role.

FIX THE INFRASTRUCTURE

The contents of this book may have surprised you as the subjects herein have focused less on the glitz and glamour and more on the foundation needed to survive the unnatural state that is fame. I purposely spent much of my focus on personal growth, because a life in the spotlight is a very public life that needs the support of a strong, mature private life for success. The people you see who seem to have it all together may be faking it, or perhaps they really have done the personal work required for such stability. The people who have had stellar, long-lasting careers in the spotlight are private realm masters from whom we can learn. That's what it takes to make it and sustain. Your public life is an extension of your private life. Even if you hide your private difficulties, you can only wear the mask for so long. What is underneath always seems to rise to the top eventually. So, before you pursue fame, at least remember these two concepts if nothing else: live from your roots of regulation and maintain a healthy life balance.

Live From Your Roots of Regulation

Your roots of regulation are who you are and what you believe. They are the rock of intuition that guides you, anchors you, and keeps you in touch with reality. Make your decisions from these roots. Don't try to be someone you're not, and don't get behind anything you don't believe in. Fame will constantly challenge you in these areas. Be strong and make decisions based on your fundamental core values. If you do that, you are more likely to be proud of the decisions you made.

You will encounter many choices as to what you will or will not say or do, and there will be many other rational reasons why you should conform to the desires of others. However, "your creativity, your intuition, and your talents are all gifts that should be enriched but never dominated by the cultural order."[1] The moment at which society tells you what to do is the moment at which you have become imprisoned by this world. "Albert Einstein called the intuitive or metaphoric mind a sacred gift. He added that the rational mind was a faithful servant...However, we have begun to worship the servant and defile the divine."[2] Trust the intuitive ability that has been granted to you by the divine. That is the sanity that keeps you from blowing away in the uncontrollable wind storm that is fame. The perils of fame are real, and celebrity will send the most mentally strong individual off the edge into reclusion, drug overdose, maladaptive sexual behavior, criminal activity, insurmountable debt, nervous breakdowns, suicide, or any number of other catastrophic events.

Maintain A Healthy Life Balance

Life balance is about developing a solid foundation and allowing those values to permeate throughout all the other aspects of your life. It is managing your life in a way that allows for all of its components to not only to line up with your roots, but also receive the constant attention needed to maintain stability. When my life has been balanced, that is when I have seen the greatest results. I'm not going to lie; it can be very hard. Life balance at its peak, like fame, like money, is a perfection that is unreachable. You can only strive to be the best you can be and find satisfaction in a fervent effort.

     Even at the writing of this book, I feel unprepared for fame, lacking in all of the subjects I have discussed, greatly in over half of them. Maintaining balance can be scary and overwhelming, and this book is helping me to understand the road ahead as much as it is hopefully helping you. Juggling all the topics covered in here is difficult enough in the dark. Doing it in the spotlight, in front of the world, compounds the situations to the greatest degree, because growth is not pretty. You take two steps forward, then one step back. You look great one day, and then the next day, you fall flat on your face. But, all you can do is get back up. You have to be resilient for fame and keep trying. Even if you have to take baby steps and tackle one thing at a time, strive for balance in your life. The more stable you are, the brighter and longer your star can shine.

     Now, with the term balance, I don't mean to always play it safe and not take any risks. In fact, if you want to be famous, you will probably need to take more risks than others normally take. Don't think that balance means boring. To get on stage, you must be willing to put yourself out there. **You must be willing to fail in order to succeed**. Instead, balance refers to recognizing your needs and taking the time to give attention to every area of your life. Fame is a spotlight, and spotlights can be blinding to the performer, but expository to the audience. The public constantly criticizes stars, but they don't understand how the distractions of fame create a breeding ground for neglect that leads to instability.

Balance, however, is an effort to handle yourself, not an effort to handle fame. If fame were an object, it would be bigger than you, it would travel faster than you, and it would live longer than you. We are truly conceited if we think that we can control such an unruly volatile experience. We can't. We are just people, and if such greatness is bestowed upon us, we can only contain so much of it before it overwhelms us. **Fame is like riding a bull: you can never totally control it; you just hold on for as long as you can**.

ARRANGE THE COURSE OF ACTION

If there is one thing that has surprised me on the road of fame, it is the level of planning involved. Even now with help, I still spend about 90% of my time planning in the dark and about 10% performing in the light. Fame doesn't just happen, and an overnight success is just the immediate illumination of a plan crafted carefully behind the scenes. You have to make a plan, or you will fail. When developing your plan for fame, you should address the three key issues of significance, support, and sustenance, with the perspective of your audience and not only yourself. The spotlight is not only an experience, and today you must think of fame as a business that requires the concentrated efforts of many people.

Significance

I thought talent was enough, but I thought wrong. Talent definitely helps, but there are scores of talented people who are not famous. Likewise, there are many famous people who appear to lack talent. **Talent is about ability, but fame is about awareness**. To get into the realm of fame, something has to lift you up before the eyes of many, sometimes regardless of your talent. If talent were a space shuttle, fame would be the rocket boosters that propel you into orbit. There are many spaceships on the ground, yet there are few comparatively flying through the air.

With so much competition and easy access to a worldwide audience via technology, drawing attention is not easy these days. You have to either build a platform or gain access to an already established platform and be ready to present an attractive product. A strong support system, money, visual stimulation, uniqueness, emotional appeal, and connections to influential people may all have to play a role in addition to your talent in order to increase your fame. But, you not only have to get people to notice. You have to get people to care, to move to action (e.g. buy your music, attend your movie premier, or support your cause) and then continue to care after their initial experience. You must significantly contribute to the life of others in order to turn your audience from casual fans to devoted followers. The value or apparent value that you offer initiates the exchange that increases your fame in return and eventually creates seeds of significance.

Support

Devoted friends, family, and hired workers will all need to play a part in launching you into the spotlight, because being famous is not a one-man show. Celebrity requires a team of people working together to uplift one person or a group of people. You will need initial supporters who can create a grassroots buzz about you throughout the community, volunteer their time and ideas, give you seed capital, and provide advice and personal life stabilization. Their enthusiasm will be contagious, and many others will notice you because of them. Your track record of a quality product and excited fans will then open the door for further opportunities.

As we saw in the last chapter, money is essential for high-level sustained fame. Again, I recommend a more stable investment as a funding source, but when you are just starting out, an even more typical and stable income flow may be needed in the form of a day job. And, a common dilemma that arises for fame seekers is whether or not a day job is initially feasible and necessary to support their fame endeavors. There are several pros and cons for each side, and I have experienced both situations, but the support of a day job is really a personal preference that is dependent on your particular circumstance.

I used to be adamantly against the day job, but I have had a change of heart in this area. When I graduated from college, I applied to every kind of music industry job I could find. However, each employer would either not hire me or request that I ride the free labor train as an intern. Neither helped my financial situation, so I gave up on the idea of having a day job altogether. I started my own music company instead and never looked back. I loved the freedom to make my own schedule and the control I had over my own career. On the other hand, I noticed several other downsides to self-employment. I always *had* to work. I was under greater pressure to make money immediately and continuously, and I began to lower my standards more and more if the money was right. There were no holidays, no days off, and few vacations. There was no consistency, only instability. One month, I would make more money than I could spend. The next month, I would make next to nothing. This turned my life into a roller coaster experience in which I was always worried about the next dollar and unable to make any concrete plans.

Unsteadiness is a common attribute of famous life, especially for artistic undertakings. Instability is part of the deal, and it takes a special kind of temperament to navigate these choppy waters. Creativity, however, requires some amount of instability, not knowing what will happen next. For at its fruition, it is lightning in a bottle. The troublesome part for most people, however, is that once you decide to play with lightning, you have to be willing to get struck a few times until you get it right.

Another interesting phenomenon occurred when I decided to do music full time. I sadly saw my zeal for it wane year after year when it was all that I did. When my passion became my job, I grew less passionate about it. I would try to explain it to people, but they just couldn't understand. They thought I had the best job in the world, but they failed to realize that their recreation was my work. And, no matter how fun it seemed, it was always work to me, gradually becoming more mundane and routine. I had a serious dilemma on my hands. If I wasn't having fun, and I wasn't making money, then why exactly was I doing this?

Eventually, I shut everything down and quit music entirely. I also experimented with my situation and discovered that I might be more suited for the steadiness of a day job. I needed a stability to counter my creativity, and when I achieved that, my security, productivity, and overall happiness improved. There was a shift in my perception. My fame wasn't an all-day-every-day drudge. It became the play time I was awarded after a hard day of work. Along with a steady stream of income, my job also provided a steady stream of repetition that denied my personal creativity just long enough for it to flourish when given the opportunity to roam free.

Sustenance

In your planning, you should always look to grow from survival to sustainability. The survival mentality is a mentality of the poor. I know it all too well, because that is how I grew up. It is a life of constant ups and downs. You make it to the next week, the next paycheck, the next gig, and you are OK…for a while. But soon after, you are back in the same rut.

If you are in a survival situation, you may tend to blame society, others, or God, but in reality, you can often bring this on yourself by choosing to remain at the low standard of survival. At some point, someone offered you survival, and you took it. Now, taking survival is not the problem; however, staying there and making survival mode a way of life is a problem you should overcome if you want to have control of your life in the spotlight.

For example, when I started a new search for a day job, I was willing to take anything that came along. I was in survival mode, and that was OK. However, once I achieved a certain level of stability in that mode, I immediately began the journey to sustainability. Instead of living in survival, I mentally determined that my survival job was temporary, and I began looking for a better-paying job. I set a standard for myself and would only accept a strict payment minimum. I turned down jobs left and right, no matter what they were for, if they only paid me enough to be in survival mode.

Even after obtaining the better paying job, I began saving large portions of my paycheck to finance my fame and create investments (this book included) that would allow me to live in the volatility of creativity more easily, maintaining a safety net to catch any blunders. That is the essence of sustainability, continual growth, bigger, better, greater. Survival looks at the here and now, but sustainability looks at the big picture. Survival asks, "What do I have today in order to make it to tomorrow?" Sustainability asks, "What do I have today that will enable me to live my dream for the rest of my life?"

At a low point in my life, I was poor and always saw the poor around me. As I heard them speak, always scheming to make a buck here or a buck there, I noticed this survival mentality that many of them had. They always said, "If I can just make it to next week…," or "If I can just pay my rent this week…" They never saw past the next day or the next week. Meanwhile, I was writing this book, thinking years ahead to today when you would read these words. **I saw then that most people don't have money problems; they have vision problems**. What mentality do you have in regards to your fame? Is it all about today or tomorrow? Can you only see what is popular this week? Or, have you thought about your sustenance 10, 20, or 30 years down the road.

A successful life in the spotlight requires that you move beyond survival. Survival suggests a lack of control. Some outside influence is persistently threatening you, and you have to combat it to survive. Sustainability, on the other hand, suggests that you are in control. You are envisioning and creating your own destiny despite the circumstances and implementing a plan in which that destiny may be fulfilled throughout your life. **Survival is visionless; sustainability is visionary**. The survival mentality is desperation, and with desperation, your priorities change. You will do anything to get what you are going after, making you a prime candidate for manipulation. Hollywood is full of desperate people who are being manipulated by others. Don't become one of them. Don't live to survive. Live to sustain.

The difference between surviving and sustaining is one reason why I don't like the terminology *struggling artist*. It denotes a pitiful state of continual failure that I will not accept. **Survival is a failure mentality. Sustainability is a famous mentality. I'm not struggling to survive. Instead, I'm striving to sustain**! In a mode of sustainability, you are building something. You are laying the foundation for a dream that is destined to be fulfilled. Survival, however, is a dream killer. And, the easiest way to see which mode you are in is to ask yourself a simple question. Why? Why do you do the things you do? Why are you chasing fame? Are you trying to make a dollar for a fix or a difference for the future?

MASTER THE DIFFICULTIES

The road you are on or the road ahead of you will be difficult. You will hurt, you will lose, you will be rejected, and you will be hated. If you want to live in the spotlight, you are not signing up for an easy task. Your troubles can even begin to make you hate your own craft. Even for me, I never thought music, the love of my life, would be counted amongst my many heartbreaks. But, if you are truly doing what you have been called to do, then you are equipped to handle what comes along. If you are destined to lead a life in the spotlight, then you are a leader, and leaders have vision. They see things in a way that most other people don't see, and this perspective is the key to overcoming every obstacle you face. **One of the keys to winning the fame game is understanding that every apparent obstacle is really several hidden opportunities**.

We all fail, and there are no perfect people. But, the person who can view their downfall with an opportunistic eye and turn problems into successes will never be truly defeated. That is an ultimate creativity which will enable you to always win. This may be difficult for you to fathom, because we naturally think in black and white, hero and villain, win and lose. But, the people who stopped pursuing their dreams are the people who saw a big obstacle and gave up. **When you reach an obstacle, life is not trying to stop you; it's trying to show you something**. Search for the truth that you are to learn, and use that truth to flip that obstacle into an opportunity.

For example, I used to play keyboards at a church. They had a B3 organ there as well, but I didn't know how to play an organ at the time, so I never touched it. Instead, I brought my keyboard every Sunday and set it up next to the organ. Well, one day my keyboard was stolen, and needless to say, that was a huge obstacle. How could I be a keyboardist without a keyboard? At the time, I didn't have enough money for a new one, and I didn't know anyone who had a decent keyboard that I could borrow. So, I was stuck...or was I?

This obstacle actually presented me with an opportunity to finally learn how to play the organ. I began to realize that the organ was also actually an obstacle in my life that I just avoided. I would miss out on jobs because I didn't know how to play it. And, I never learned because I never had a teacher or access to an organ. Well, now that I had access, there was one more hurdle to overcome. I still had no teacher, but I overcame that as well by using every resource available to me. I read books, manuals, and internet articles. I watched videos and attended concerts. I talked to people who played so that they could give me tips. And, within a week I could play the organ! Within a few weeks, I was proficient. I enhanced the music at the church, I learned how to play a new instrument, and I increased my value and my expertise for any further musical positions. My obstacle became several opportunities, and it all started with how I viewed the situation.

It would be great if the level of fame you dream of and plan for just happens. However, life tends to have a way of rerouting you, and the harsh reality is that statistically speaking, your chances of fame on a high level are slim to none. The fame scale is actually more like a pyramid. The bottom is broad with many people, but the top is narrow with a few. Logically speaking, it is impossible for everyone to be at the top, but is that failure for the millions of people who don't achieve that goal? That is the question I have wrestled with for years. Even if fame is less of a destination and more of a sliding scale, you still tend to want to be as high on that scale as possible. So, if you want to be famous on that high level but it does not happen for you, then what do you do?

After contemplating this dilemma, I realized that there are five options for when things don't work out the way you think they should. However, to understand those five scenarios, you must understand the differences and relationships between goals and paths. Your goal is your destination. It is the prize you desire and the focus of your efforts. Goals can remain firm, they can change completely, or they can evolve over time. Paths, on the other hand, are the methods you use to achieve your goals. Just like goals, paths can change; however, paths tend to change more rapidly and are more influenced by outside factors. In comparison, goals tend to be steadfast and held to more dearly.

In relation to your fame, there may be many paths to a goal or many goals for a path. A plant, for instance, is an awesome natural example of this. Obtaining sunlight and water are two natural goals of a plant. Even if you put a maze in its way, a plant will grow in the path of the maze that will bring it to sunlight and water. Because of the obstacle in its way, the plant alters its normal path so that it still can attain its goal. Let's look at a few more situational examples so that you can see all five scenarios at work.

1. Persistence: Same Goal, Same Path

David wants to be a millionaire, but he hates risky investments. He plans on achieving his millionaire status through saving a little bit every month. Despite economic changes, differing opinions from associates and other obstacles, he remains focused. On his 92nd birthday, he becomes a millionaire, and his story is featured on a television special.

2. Ingenuity: Same Goal, Different Path

Ashley's goal is to be a great dancer. One day, however, she is struck by a car and loses the ability to walk. But, instead of relinquishing her initial goal, she strengthens her arms and participates in a wheelchair dance ensemble that captivates audiences around the world.

3. Wisdom: Different Goal, Same Path

Jordan wants to be a famous hip hop artist, but no one attends his concerts and his records never sell. He acknowledges the poor results of his performance and stops pursuing that dream, but other successful performers begin to take interest in his writing ability. He shifts his focus from the performance to the pen and eventually becomes one of hip hop's most sought-after ghostwriters.

4. Courage: Different Goal, Different Path

Miguel wants to be an actor. However, his work calls for long hours and an unstable schedule. His job is affecting his ability to be a good husband and father, and with his third child on the way, he expects things to get worse. So, Miguel goes back to school to get his MBA. He works his way up to become the president of a large corporation and is now featured in numerous magazines across the country.

5. Failure: No Goal, No Path

Emma wants to be a movie star, but everyone passes her up, and she never obtains a role. So, she not only gives up on movies, she also gives up on life and stops having any kind of dreams or goals for herself. She just sits at home now doing nothing.

When artist friends of mine struggled or felt like failures, I always told them to never give up. At that time, the only option I knew was to maintain the same goal and the same path with the idea that if you do not give up, you will eventually succeed. But as I grew older and experienced more of the hardships of life, I realized that I may have given bad advice. I saw that sadly **you are never promised success just because you keep trying**.

Considering the five fame options, I now believe that your response to a situation in which it appears that your original goal or path may not be realized can only be right or wrong based on your individual convictions. I cannot fault David in Example 1 because he was determined to remain steadfast with the same goal and same path. That is the admirable quality of persistence which could have inspired countless people whether he reached his goal or not. Similarly, I can find no fault with Ashley in Example 2. She not only had the determination to keep her same goal despite the circumstances, but also the ingenuity to find a path that would allow her to accomplish that goal. In Example 3, Jordan's ability to recognize that he was using the right method for the wrong goal was a sign of personal development, selflessness, wisdom, and maturity. And, in Example 4, it took a great deal of humility for Miguel to put his family first. In addition, going back to school in a totally different field exemplified the courage it takes to get out and try something completely different. The scenario you choose for yourself is totally up to you. You must make your own choice for your own life. Think critically about your career and seek the advice of your inner circle. When you feel restless, disinterested, annoyed, disappointed, inefficient, or unstable, it may be time for a new goal and/or path.

The fifth example is the saddest, and it is the only condition where I see immediate failure. Emma completely gave up on life, on growth, on forward progress, and that is death. The sure way to lose at the fame game is to quit before the game is over. Life will always throw change at you. You can adjust, or you can give up. Life's changes are not always the brick walls that we think they are. Often, they are hurdles. You can either stop or jump over. In the first four examples, everyone jumped. However, Emma just stopped. **There's a difference between giving up on your life and giving in to change**. There's a difference between quitting and adapting. The people who adapt are the ones who survive long enough to sustain. They are the ones who win.

I would love to say that there is a secret formula that turns you into the next superstar, but there isn't one. There are numerous things outlined in this book that you can do to help your cause, but life is too unpredictable, and fame is too fickle. For the people at the top, life just has to work out in a near perfect manner for them. You, on the other hand, may start off heading to point A and a few years down the road, end up at point D. However, there may be precious opportunity within the unexpected outcome, and **you can thrive if you take advantage of your circumstance rather than be consumed by it**. I always imagined myself being famous in music, and I never saw myself extending into any other art forms. I felt so lost when suddenly I wanted to quit music altogether. Life just took me down some different roads, and I have had to make adjustments. The same may happen to you.

ESTABLISH THE DEEP CONNECTION

I have often found that to obtain what you are truly seeking in life, you must first do the opposite. In order to receive you must give; in order to go up, you must first go down. Now, if you just want to be purely selfish in your quest for fame, then just do something eye-catching and different. Do anything and everything that will attract attention to you. You will attract a crowd, but you will have no relationship with them. You will have not connected deeply with them, and they will not connect deeply with you. However, if you want your fame to be long-lasting; if you want to go past the fruit into the seeds of significance; if you want the fifth E of having an effect on people, you need to establish a deep connection. In order to impact many, you must first turn a few into fans or fanatics. Don't just sell to them. Don't just use them. They are people, not stepping stones. If you really want to be remembered in the hearts and minds of many, then after you attract fans, you need to give to them. Support them, listen to them, love them, show them that you care, and empower them to spread your fame through the significance you have established.

RESPECT THE JOURNEY

Fame is an ongoing process, not a place; it's a journey, not a destination. People don't automatically become famous. You may not see it, but there is always a process involved. It is important to respect the journey that you are on, because respecting each phase that you go through enables you to enjoy and learn. The stars, however, who do not mature during the process of stardom are the ones who tend to flame out.

Take a step back, enlarge your perspective, and evaluate your achievements. Hold onto anything that marks significant milestones in your life. Build on that and encourage yourself. Simultaneously, strive for a better future, but seek peace concerning your present situation. We can spend so much of our lives looking forward to future events that we miss out on the beauty of our present circumstance. **If fame becomes too much of an obsession, you'll waste the life you have by chasing the life you want**. Value yourself and value your uniqueness. Remember, no one has been or will ever be quite like you. No one has had or will ever have the journey you have had.

We often get tricked into believing that there is some magical point in our lives where we will have arrived. However, the subjective nature of fame makes it extremely difficult to quantify. I know this sounds cliché, but in reality, the future is *now*. Saying what you will be or what you are going to do constantly reinforces the idea that you have not arrived, that there is something missing, and that you are not worthwhile until you reach that point. It swings open the door for procrastination and can leave you feeling like a depressed, unfulfilled individual who hasn't accomplished anything. You should not say, "I will be." Instead, you should say, "I am." Declare for the present, not for the future. Once you declare, you are. When you say, "I will," you act because you said. But, when you say, "I am," you act because you are. "I will" is a straight line with a start and an end. "I am" is a circle of continuous being. When you say, "I will," in your doing, you are chasing your words. But, when you say, "I am," in your doing, you are confirming your words.

Fame is like a road trip; the fun experiences on the road often become much more memorable than the destination. So, no matter what happens to you, respect the unique journey that you have been given and do your best, because you never know who is watching you and being inspired by you. In fact, you are probably more famous now than you think you are. Sociologists claim that an average person can influence 10,000 people in their lifetime, even if they are introverted![3] By the time you read this, you will have already probably affected thousands of people whether you realize it or not. People are watching you, you are famous right now, and you should proceed accordingly.

We see the same stories over and over again, yet we don't learn from the mistakes. Daily, manipulators are taking advantage of people who are desperate for the spotlight. Many have experienced identity crises and physical disorders; mental, social, and emotional issues and breakdowns; ungrounded immoral states; exposed private matters; poorly-managed public images; scandalous events; business blunders; and financial woes. These are the issues I have addressed here in this book so that you may know the traps and pitfalls that lie in your pathway.

I have given you a road map, but it's up to you to use it. **Good things may come to those who wait, but the spotlight shines on those who work**. Your job, however, is less of trying to figure out ways to get to the important people. Instead, you should focus on figuring out ways to make the important people want to come to you. If you want to make it, you have to establish your identity. You have to know who you are and what you stand for. You need to work on your physical presentation so that you communicate the right messages and are able to handle the rigorous demands of a famous life. You have to be aware of your mental, emotional, social and spiritual health; take control of personal matters; and separate the darkness from the spotlight. Only you can have the foundation to overcome your scandals and learn from scams. You have to be professional in business and wise with your money. And, lastly, you have to be flexible enough to adapt to change, having the discernment to accept both failure and new opportunities.

If you can address these issues early on, your road will be much smoother than those of many other celebrities. But in any case, don't become paranoid. If you fall, it's OK. The allegoric hero always has a weakness. We all fall, but the key is rebounding. **If you continue to rise, you will continue to win**. Remember...

> The fastest runner doesn't always win the race, and the strongest warrior doesn't always win the battle. The wise sometimes go hungry, and the skillful are not necessarily wealthy. And those who are educated don't always lead successful lives. It is all decided by chance, by being in the right place at the right time.[4]

If you just hoist your kite, you will fly, but the wind will ultimately determine how high you go. Don't wait for fame. Your story has already begun. You don't become famous; you are always being famous!

Works Cited

1 (Samples 62)

2 (Samples 26)

3 (Elmore)

4 (*NLT*, Eccl. 9:11)

BIBLIOGRAPHY

"50 Famous People With Depression, Mental Illness." *WCVB-TV5*. Hearst Stations, Inc., n.d. Web. 29 Jun. 2016.

ABC Television Network. *I.T.R.S Ranking Report. ABC Medianet*. American Broadcasting Companies, Inc., 31 May 2006. Web 29 Jan. 2015.

Adams, William Lee. "The Dark Side of Creativity: Depression + Anxiety Madness = Genius?" *CNN Style*. Cable News Network. Turner Broadcasting Systems, Inc., n.d. Web. 28 Jun. 2016.

ADVICEFORLIVING. "Mandy More Talks To Mel Robbins About Saying No." *YouTube*. YouTube, 29 Jan. 2010. Web. 3 Feb. 2015.

Allen Rachael. "Stalin and the Great Terror: Can Mental Illness Explain Violent Behavior?" Guided History. *Guided History*, n.d. Web. 29 Jun. 2016.

Alliance for Audited Media. Alliance for Audited Media, 30 Jun. 2014. Web. 29 Jan. 2015.

"Anne Hathaway: 'There's Something Very Addictive About People-Pleasing.'" *Extra*. Telepictures Productions, Inc., 28 Jun. 2011. Web. 3 Feb. 2015.

Avalon, Moses. "What Are The Vegas Odds Of Success On Today's Major Label Record Deal?" *Moses Avalon*. The Moses Avalon Company, 29 Jun. 2011. Web. 31 Jan. 2015.

Borges, Anna. "17 Celebrities Who Opened Up About Mental Health In 2015." *Buzzfeed*. Buzzfeed, Inc., 8 Dec. 2015. Web. 29 Jun. 2016.

Borkowski, Mark. *The Fame Formula: How Hollywood's Fixers, Fakers and Star Makers Created the Celebrity Industry*. London: Sidgwick & Jackson, 2008. Print.

Braudy, Leo. *The Frenzy of Renown: Fame & Its History*. New York: Oxford UP, 1986. Print.

"'Bride Of Wildenstein' Who Famously Spent $4million On Plastic

Surgery Cleared By Court To Remain In Her Trump Tower Apartment After Settling $73,500 Rent Row With Landlord." *Daily Mail*. Associated Newspapers Ltd., 2 Feb. 2013 Web 3 Feb. 2015.

Bryan, William Jennings and Bryan, Mary (Baird). *The Memoirs of William Jennings Bryan*. Philadelphia: The John C. Winston Company, c1925. Print.

Cameron, Julia. *The Artist's Way: A Spiritual Path to Higher Creativity*. Los Angeles, CA: Jeremy P. Tarcher/Perigee, 1992. Print.

Celzic, Mike. "Miss South Carolina Teen USA Explains Herself." *Today*. NBCNews.com. 28 Aug. 2007. Web. 4 Feb. 2015.

Covey, Stephen R. *The 7 Habits of Highly Effective People: Restoring the Character Ethic*. New York: Free, 2004. Print.

Cronin, Melissa. "Creativity Tied To Mental Illnesses Like Bipolar Disorder, Schizophrenia In New Swedish Study." *The Huffington Post*, 17 Oct. 2012. Web. 31 Jan. 2015.

Cross, Charles R. *Room Full of Mirrors: A Biography of Jimi Hendrix*. New York: Hyperion, 2005. Print.

Dimensional Research. "Customer Service and Business Results: A Survey of Customer Service From Mid-Size Companies." Zendesk, Apr. 2013. Web. 2 Feb. 2015.

Dunn, Elizabeth and Michael Norton. "Don't Indulge. Be Happy." *The New York Times*. The New York Times Company, 7 Jul. 2012. Web. 4 Apr. 2015.

Elmore, Tim. "Is Everyone A Leader?" *Psychology Today*. Sussex Publishers, LLC, 20 Feb. 2014. Web. 4 Apr. 2015.

"Episode 307." *Shark Tank*. ABC. KABC, Los Angeles. 3 Mar. 2012. Television.

Facebook, Inc. *Facebook Reports Fourth Quarter and Full Year 2013 Results*. PR Newswire. PR Newswire Association, LLC, 29 Jan. 2014. Web. 29

Jan. 2015.

"Fame." *Merriam-Webster.com*. Merriam Webster's Learner's Dictionary, n.d. Web. 3 Jun. 2014.

Flamm, Matthew. *Crain's New York Business*. Crain Communications, Inc., 10 Jan. 2012. Web. 29 Jan. 2015.

"Flash Facts About Lightning." *National Geographic News*. National Geographic Society, 24 June 2005. Web. 18 May 2016.

Flocker, Michael. *The Fame Game: How to Make the Most of Your 15 Minutes*. Cambridge, MA: Da Capo, 2005. Print.

Gawain, Shakti, and Laurel King. *Living in the Light*. Mill Valley, CA: Whatever Pub., 1986. Print.

Ghebremedhin, Sabina, et al. "Exclusive: Inside Hollywood's 'Bling Ring.'" *ABC News*. ABC News Internet Ventures, 3 Mar. 2010. Web. 4 Feb. 2015.

Holmes, Oliver Wendell. "The Voiceless." *The Poetical Works of Oliver Wendell Holmes*. London: G. Routledge, 1852. Print.

House, Laurel, and Sharon House. *The Gurus' Guide to Serenity: A Me-time Menu of Celebrity Stress Reducers*. New York: W. Morrow, 2004. Print.

Kavoussi, Bonnie. "Half of Americans Are Spending More Than They Earn, But Don't Realize It: Survey." *The Huffington Post*. TheHuffingtonPost.com, Inc., 17 May 2012. Web. 30 Mar. 2015.

Kelley, Raina. "10 Celebrities Who Got In Hot Water With The IRS." Business Insider. Business Insider, Inc., 7 Mar. 2012. Web. 18 Mar. 2015.

Kiyosaki, Robert T., and Sharon L. Lechter. *Rich Dad, Poor Dad: What the Rich Teach Their Kids About Money – That the Poor and Middle Class Do Not!* New York: Warner Business, 2000. Print.

Lewis, Katherine. "About Katherine." *Harmony and Balance*. Harmony and Balance, Inc., n.d. Web. 2 Feb. 2015.

Lopez, Cory. "Sofia Vergara Trying To Block Sale Of Stolen Photos: 15 Stars Who've Been Hacked (GALLERY)." *Celebuzz*. SpinMedia, n.d. Web. 4 Feb. 2015.

Macnab, Geoffrey. "I Know How To Be A Star." *The Guardian*. Guardian News and Media Limited, 31 Dec. 2003. Web. 4 Apr. 2015.

"Marilyn Monroe Lets Her Hair Down About Being Famous." *Life*. 3 Aug. 1962: 38 Print.

Martinez, Jose, David Whitley, and Ralph Warner. "Big Poppas: The Athletes With The Most Children By The Most Women." *Complex*. Complex Media Inc., 17 Jan. 2012. Web. 18 Mar. 2015.

Maslow, A.H. "A Theory Of Human Motivation." *Psychological Review* 50. (1943): 370-96. Print.

McGuiness, Kristen. "Are Celebrities More Prone To Addiction?" *The Fix*. The Fix, 18 Jan. 2012. Web. 4 Feb. 2015.

Mehrabian, Albert. "Silent Messages." *Personality & Communication: Psychological Books & Articles of Popular Interest*. Albert Mehrabian, n.d. Web. 31 Jan. 2015.

"Michael Jackson Died Deeply In Debt." Billboard. Billboard, 26 Jun. 2009. Web. 18 Mar. 2015.

Monroe, Marilyn, and Roger Taylor. *Marilyn Monroe In Her Own Words*. New York: Delilah/Putnam, 1983. Print.

Montag, Heidi, and Spencer Pratt. *How to Be Famous: Our Guide to Looking the Part, Playing the Press, and Becoming a Tabloid Fixture*. New York: Grand Central Pub., 2009. Print.

"Neology" Def. 1. *Merriam Webster Online*. Merriam Webster, n.d. Web. 4 Feb. 2015.

People In Sports. "35 Athletes With Depression." *Ranker*. Ranker, Inc., n.d. Web. 28 Jun. 2016.

Petronzio, Matt. "U.S. Adults Spend 11 Hours Per Day With Digital Media." *Mashable*. Mashable, Inc., 5 Mar. 2014. Web. 20 May 2016.

Reality TV World. Reality TV World, n.d. Web. 29 Jan. 2015.

"Review Of Research Challenges Assumption That Success Makes People Happy: Happiness May Lead To Success Via Positive Emotions." *American Psychological Association*. American Psychological Association, 18 Dec. 2005. Web. 3 Feb. 2015.

Rutenberg, Jim. "The Gossip Machine, Churning Out Cash." *The New York Times* 21 May 2011: A1. Web. 14 Sep. 2014.

Samples, Bob. *The Metaphoric Mind: A Celebration of Creative Consciousness*. Reading, MA: Addison-Wesley Pub., 1976. Print.

Smith, Siobhan. "How Musicians Are Breaking Down The Stigma Of Mental Illness." *Wow247*. Johnston Publishing Ltd., 26 Oct. 2015. Web. 28 Jun. 2016.

"Social Skills" Def.1. *CollinsDictionary.com*. Harper Collins Publishers, n.d. Web. 4 Feb. 2015.

"Spin Control" Def. 1. *Merriam Webster Online*. Merriam Webster, n.d. Web. 10 Mar. 2015.

"Spirituality." *Medical Reference Guide*. University of Maryland Medical System, n.d. Web. 2 Feb. 2015.

Stein, Garth. *The Art of Racing in the Rain: A Novel*. New York: Harper, 2008. Print.

Stibich, Mark. "Top 10 Reasons To Smile." *About*. About.com. IAC, 16 Dec. 2014. Web. 31 Jan. 2015.

"Style." Def. 2. *Merriam-Webster.com*. Merriam Webster's Learner's Dictionary, n.d. Web. 7 Apr. 2013.

"Sued Celebs." *DailyNews.com*. Daily News, L.P., n.d. Web. 4 Feb. 2015.

The Global Language Monitor. The Global Language Monitor, 1 Jan. 2014. Web. 4 Feb. 2015.

The Holy Bible, New International Version. Biblica, Inc., 2011. Web.

The Holy Bible, New Living Translation. Tyndale House Publishers, Inc., 2007. Web.

The Notorious B.I.G. "Mo Money Mo Problems." *Life After Death*. Bad Boy Records/Arista Records, 1997. CD.

Thorn, Craig. "14 Comedians You Didn't Know Suffered From Depression." *The Richest*. TheRichest.com, 12 May 2014. Web. 28 Jun. 2016.

"Vanilla Ice." *Bio*. A&E Television Networks, 2015. Web. 2 Feb. 2015.

Warren, Rick. "Principles Of Leadership: Meditation and Relaxation." *Leadership Lifters*. Purpose Driven Small Group Network, 29 May 2010. Web. 2 Feb. 2015.

"When Fans Attack! Celebrities Who've Had Frightening Fan Encounters In Concert!" *Perezhilton.com*. Perezhilton.com, n.d. Web. 4 Feb. 2015.

"Why Would You Want To Be Famous." *BBC News*. BBC, 4 Apr. 2003. Web. 3 Feb. 2015.

Williams, Tia. "Tax Season Porn: 34 Stars Who Made Bazillions And Went Bankrupt." *VH1*. Viacom Media Networks., 13 Mar. 2013. Web. 18 Mar. 2015.

Winograd, David. "Charles Koch Foundation: An Income Of $34,000 Puts You In The Wealthiest 1 Percent." *The Huffington Post*. TheHuffingtonPost.com, Inc., 11 Jul. 2013. Web. 18 Mar. 2015.

YouTube LLC, "Press Room - YouTube." *YouTube*. YouTube LLC, n.d. Web. 29 Jan. 2015

ABOUT THE AUTHOR

Zap Rath is a creative artist and no stranger to fame. In junior high school, he completed a 3-year guitar course in an unprecedented 2 years. That was followed by a solo concert for the entire school, after which he signed autographs. He also learned to play nearly a dozen musical instruments before finishing high school, achieving another unprecedented school record by winning on four different instruments in a single competition.

Zap is also a graduate of the University of Southern California with honors including nominations for two awards from the American Black Music Association and invitations from President Bill Clinton and President George Bush, Jr. to attend the National Young Leadership Conference and Global Young Leadership Conference in Washington D.C. and Australia, respectively.

With professional experience as a musician, music director, music producer, music instructor, singer, rapper, stage manager, audio engineer, record label assistant, comedian, dancer, actor, model, public speaker, marketing specialist, salesman, entrepreneur, and now author, he is the perfect candidate to write a book of this nature. After researching fame and celebrity life for years, *Being Famous* is sure to be the next jewel in his crown of achievements.

FAME ADVISOR
www.fameadvisor.com
Join For FREE Today!

Now that you've read *Being Famous*, you understand just how difficult it is to attain and sustain fame. We know that this can be a bit overwhelming, and that's why we created Fame Advisor to be your number one source for support on your journey through fame. Get an edge over the competition by taking advantage of Fame Advisor's membership benefits, including…

Helpful Articles and Videos
Prizes, Drawings, and Giveaways
Exclusive Events
Members Only Forums
Personal Fame Consultation
Discounted Products
Promotional Opportunities
Live Webinars
Fame Monitoring With FameScore™
Q&A With Experienced Fame Advisors
And more!

Facebook: Fame Advisor   Twitter/Instagram: @fameadvisor

Has this book helped you? Email us today, and tell us about it!
Who knows? We may feature your story!

Email: info.benbooks@gmail.com